Editor
Tom Finley

Assistant Editor
Lauren Ajer

Consulting Editors
Marian Wiggins
Annette Parrish

Contributing Writers
Rick Bundschuh
Carol Bostrom
Ed Reed
Kim Vander Linden

Designed and Illustrated by Tom Finley

The standard Bible text used in this course is the Holy Bible, *The New International Version*. Copyright © 1973, 1978, 1984 by the International Bible Society. Used by permission of Zondervan Bible Publishers.

Also used is: *NASB—The New American Standard Bible.* © The Lockman Foundation 1960, 1962, 1963, 1968, 1971, 1972, 1973, 1975. Used by permission.

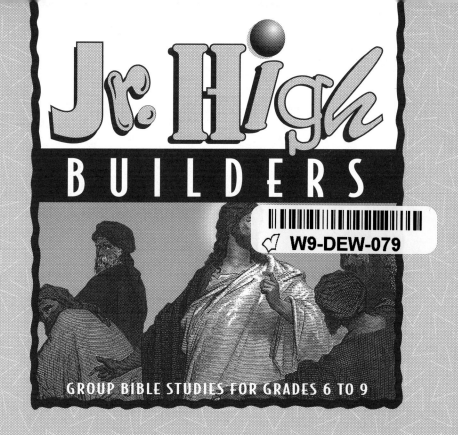

Jr. High

BUILDERS

W9-DEW-079

GROUP BIBLE STUDIES FOR GRADES 6 TO 9

THE PARABLES OF JESUS

NUMBER 3 IN A SERIES OF 12

Gospel Light

INTRODUCTION: OVERVIEW OF THE PARTS AND PIECES

This book contains everything you need to teach any size group of junior high students about many of Christ's parables. Thirteen sessions, with complete session plans for the leader, reproducible classroom worksheets and reproducible take-home sheets. Also, thirteen lecture-oriented Bible study outlines based on the same themes, to provide your students with needed reinforcement from a fresh perspective. And—dozens of action games and a special section of clip art featuring illustrations to promote your Bible studies and dress up your announcement handbills.

Contents

The Parts and Pieces

● The **SESSION PLAN** contains two essential ingredients for a meaningful Bible study all students will enjoy: a commentary section to provide the leader with important biblical information and to set the stage for the lesson; and a lesson plan filled with Bible Learning Activities to help students retain spiritual truths.
FOR A DETAILED DESCRIPTION, TURN TO PAGE 4.

Pride and Humility
Session 3

INSIGHTS FOR THE LEADER

WHAT THE SESSION IS ABOUT
Pride can damage a Christian's life.

SCRIPTURE STUDIED
Job 32:1; Psalm 36:2; Proverbs 16:5; 27:2; Matthew 13:15; 15:8,9; Luke 18:9-14; Galatians 6:3.

KEY PASSAGE
"Everyone who exalts himself will be humbled, and he who humbles himself will be exalted." Luke 18:14

THE SESSION

This session focuses on a believer's attitudes towards others and God. These attitudes are sometimes revealed in prayer. The parable of Jesus that is examined in this session teaches proper attitudes not only in prayer but in our whole way of thinking about God. The length of prayer, the form of prayer and the proper words in prayer are not emphasized. God is not impressed with our many words or with proper form. He is concerned about our attitude of heart. People are concerned with the outward appearance of things, but God is concerned with the heart.

The Pharisee and the Tax Collector
To teach us about our heart attitude, told a parable...

ernment in Rome and who gouged the public by overcharging and keeping the excess, were considered to be on a level with robbers and murderers. By speaking of a Pharisee and a tax collector, Jesus set up a contrast between a devout religious leader and a known sinner. The questions are, who is God going to hear? Who will have his prayers answered? Who will be justified (forgiven)?

Everyone hearing of these two men would naturally conclude that the "good" man, the Pharisee, would surely be heard by God. The word "Pharisee" literally means "the separated one." The Pharisees...

2

● The **STUDENT WORKSHEET,** called the **Parchment,** allows the student to learn by doing rather than just sitting and listening. Photocopy as many sheets as you need. **SEE PAGE 6 FOR COMPLETE DETAILS.**

The Parchment SESSION 5

The Servant's Report

Read Luke 14:16-24. You are the servant asked to bring people to the feast. At the end of your day's work, fill out this report. Make sure to tell what happened and your feelings about it.

ACTIVITY LEDGER

Day ending _____ Time _____
Comments or observations

Guest #1

Guest #2

Guest #3

Invitation List

Perhaps you know some friends or relatives who need to be invited to know Christ. List them below.

PEOPLE TO INVITE TO
THE HEAVENLY BANQUET

1.
2.
3.
4.
5.

The **TEACHING RESOURCE PAGE** provides special items such as short stories or case studies when required by the **Session Plan.** Most **Session Plans** have no **Teaching Resource Page. FOR DETAILS, SEE PAGE 7.**

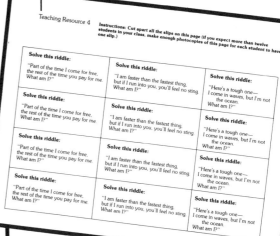

Teaching Resource 4

Instructions: Cut apart all the slips on this page (if you expect more than twelve students in your class, make enough photocopies of this page for each student to have one slip.)

Solve this riddle:
"Part of the time I come for free, the rest of the time you pay for me. What am I?"

Solve this riddle:
"I am faster than the fastest thing, but if I run into you, you'll feel no sting. What am I?"

Solve this riddle:
"Here's a tough one— I come in waves, but I'm not the ocean. What am I?"

ACME YELLOW STRING

Session 2

There's been an explosion at the "ACME YELLOW STRING" factory! With a pen or a pencil, follow the strings from each letter in the "ACME YELLOW STRING" banner below. Some of those strings dead-end off to the sides in knots, but the rest continue on down to the seven boxes at the bottom where they spell out the answer to this question.

"This must come under the Lord's control. What is it?"

A C M E Y E L L O W S T R I N G

There's a big difference between knowing what to do, and doing it. If you want to have a living, dynamic faith in God, you have to place yourself in His hands and allow Him to take charge.

DAILY NUGGETS

Day 1 Read James 1:22-25. Why is it not enough just to hear the Word?

Day 2 Colossians 3:15-17. Think of some of the things you've done recently. How many could be done in the name of the Lord and with thanksgiving?

Day 3 John 13:12-17. What did Jesus do? How ways you will serve others this week with the knew Jesus Christ.

Day 4 Mark 4:21-25. What does verse 21 teach you about letting your light shine for others to see?

Day 5 Hebrews 11:8-16. What did Abraham have that helped him do what the Lord told him to do?

Day 6 Isaiah 1:18-20. Write down the result of rebelling against God. Then write the results of obedience. Which is the better choice?

"In the same way, faith by itself, if it is not accompanied by action, is dead."

James 2:17

The **TAKE-HOME PAPER,** called the **Fun Page,** features a Bible game (such as a maze or crossword), daily devotional questions and a memory verse for motivated students. **FOR MORE ABOUT THE FUN PAGE, TURN TO PAGE 8.**

The **POPSHEET** is a lecture-oriented version of the **Session Plan,** based on a different portion of the Scriptures. Use it as an alternative to the **Session Plan,** at another meeting later in the week, or combine it with the **Session Plan** as you see fit.

POPSHEET

THE COMPLETE JUNIOR HIGH BIBLE STUDY RESOURCE BOOK #3
© 1988 GL LIGHT FORCE, VENTURA, CA 93006

THEME: To know Christ is as important as knowing about Him.

Session 1

BIBLE STUDY OUTLINE

Begin your message by reading 2 Timothy 1:11,12 to your listeners.

• The author of this passage was Paul. Paul tells us that he was suffering persecution for his beliefs. In fact, when Paul wrote these words, he was stuck in a cold dungeon, shackled in chains. Yet, as he says in verse 12, he was not ashamed. The reason he was not ashamed was because he knew whom he had believed. That is, he knew Jesus Christ.

• Notice that Paul did not say, "I know all about Christ," or, "I know why I believe." He said, "I know whom I have believed." Today there are many people who know all about Jesus. They know how to sing the songs in church and can find a few verses in the Bible. Yet many of these people simply don't know Jesus Himself. It is not enough to know about Him, you and I must know Him.

• Now let's take a look at the change in Paul's life this knowledge of Jesus made. Paul says he **knows** whom he has **believed.** The faith came because he knew Jesus. And because he **believed** in Jesus Christ, Paul was able to guard what Paul had **entrusted** to Him. It's safe to assume that Paul had entrusted his life to Jesus. Paul's faith grew to maturity, he met and got to know Jesus. And so we see a progression: Paul became convinced of Jesus power, he entrusted everything to Jesus. Everything was founded on the fact that Paul knew Jesus. You and I have to know Him, too. (At this point, the OBJECT LESSON stunt should take place.)

OBJECT LESSON:
WHAT DO YOU KNOW?

Have an adult (a stranger to your students or someone in a disguise) sneak unnoticed into the room, suddenly run up to you while shouting, push a whipped cream pie in your face and quickly run out of the room.

Wipe your face off with a towel and calm students down. Reassure them that the act was planned by you as a demonstration of an important point. Say something like, **You all saw what happened. But how many of you can accurately recall details of what just happened?** Let's find out.

Ask questions like these: What color was the person's pants (skirt, dress)? Was he or she wearing a watch? Was the person taller or shorter than me? How many seconds was the person in the room? What kind of shoes did the person wear? Which door did he or she come in? What were his or her exact words?

Probably no single person will have the answers to all the questions. In fact, some questions may stump the whole group.

Point out that, just like the students who really don't have a completely accurate knowledge of the details of this amazing incident, many Christians really don't have a clear or complete knowledge of Jesus Christ. Say, **Too many Christians just learn a few basics about Christ, but never seem to get to know Him. And knowing Jesus should be the most important thing to us.**

DISCUSSION QUESTIONS

1. What's the difference between knowing about Christ and knowing Christ?
2. How can Christians get to know Him better?
3. Will there ever be a point when we can say we know Him perfectly? Why or why not?
4. Paul says he believed, was convinced and had entrusted himself to Jesus. What do all these words mean? How can they be experienced in our own lives today?
5. Paul says he entrusted to Him that "that day." What day do you suppose that is? Is that day important to us? What happens to the person who is not prepared for that day?

THE COMPLETE JUNIOR HIGH BIBLE STUDY RESOURCE BOOK #3

GAMES & THINGS

Here are some fun things you can do with tape recorders.

AUDIO SCAVENGER HUNT

Provide teams with cassette recorders and send them into the neighborhood with adult team leaders to collect sounds. Here are some suggestions of what to look for:

A man's voice singing a verse from "I Did It My Way."
The sound of air being released from a balloon.
A gas station bell.
The sound of a cash register.
A cat's meow (or a woman imitating a cat).
A dog's bark.
Water running in a sink or bathtub.
A television commercial for food.
"Welcome to McDonald's. May I take your order please?" (Said over the drive-up intercom.)
A piano or electric guitar.

NAME THAT TUNE

...bthe all the record albums you can find (from "goldies" to current) and create several minutes worth of clips from the better-known songs. Each clip should be two to three seconds long. Play the first clip ...roup. The first person to recognize the song jumps up and is allowed to make his or her guess. A ...t scores five points, a wrong guess loses one point. Keep track of the scores.

NAME THAT SOUND

...e same as "NAME THAT TUNE," except players are to guess the source of the sounds you've recorded. In addition to some of the sounds listed in "AUDIO SCAVENGER HUNT," try:

A washing machine.
The engine of a car.
A skateboard.
The splash of someone diving into a pool.
A dog with long toenails walking on a tile floor.
A chair being shoved backward on a tile floor.

The **Popsheet** features **GAMES AND THINGS,** dozens of action games for your students to enjoy. **PAGE 10 CONTAINS DETAILS.**

The **CLIP ART AND OTHER GOODIES** section at the back of the book contains special art you can use to dress up your newsletters. **SEE PAGE 12 FOR COMPLETE INFORMATION.**

3

THE SESSION PLANS

How to squeeze the most out of each Bible study.

● **Every Session Plan contains the following features:**

1. INTRODUCTORY INFORMATION

WHAT THE SESSION IS ABOUT states the main thrust of the lesson.

Your students will examine all verses listed in **SCRIPTURE STUDIED.**

The **KEY PASSAGE** is also the memory verse given on the **Fun Page** takehome paper.

AIMS OF THE SESSION are what you hope to achieve during class time. You may wish to privately review these after class as a measure of your success.

Building by the Plans
Session 2

WHAT THE SESSION IS ABOUT
We build our Christian lives by obedience to Christ.

SCRIPTURE STUDIED
Matthew 21:28-32; James 2:14-18.

KEY PASSAGE
"In the same way, faith by itself, if it is not accompanied by action, is dead." James 2:17

AIMS OF THE SESSION
During this session your learners will:
1. Identify obedience as a main ingredient for building one's life in Christ;
2. Describe specific areas in which Christians should be obedient;
3. Select an area of obedience to put into action.

INSIGHTS FOR THE LEADER

God wants us to do what He asks. This is the thrust of the parable of the two sons which your class will be studying in this session. The parables of Jesus are just as relevant today as they were when He gave them. Boys haven't changed much! They are still having problems doing what their parents ask them to do.

This parable is the result of the questioning of Jesus' authority. Jesus had entered the city as a royal monarch. The people had lined the streets of Jerusalem blessing Him and shouting "Hosanna to the Son of David" (Matt. 21:9). He entered the Temple and, as the Lord of the Temple, He drove out those who were ma[king] it a street market "'It is written', he s[aid] them, 'My house will be called a h[ouse of] prayer,' but you are making it a 'd[en of rob]bers'" (verse 13).

By this action Jesus was cla[iming to be the] very "Lord of the Templ[e..." The] gious establi[shment...] lying down. [...] He made for [...] especially that [...] popularity they [...] actions. They h[...] by His own wor[d...] God and thus th[...] So, with subtle [...] "By what autho[rity...] things?' they asked [...] authority?'" (verse [...]

posed a question for them to answer: "John's baptism—where did it come from? Was it from heaven, or from men?" (verse 25). They could not answer, because to say "from heaven" would have given credence to John's attacks on them (see Matt. 3:7) and to say "from men" would have placed them in disfavor with the crowds.

Following this exchange, Jesus answered their question in a very clever way. He spoke of a father with two sons. The father asked his [first son to go...] [to] work. The first [...]ard to work. [...]y, but later changed his mind [...] at his father had asked. The second [...] responded, "'I will, sir,' but he [...] [21:30).

2. INSIGHTS FOR THE LEADER

This part of each lesson is background for you, the leader. Study this section with your Bible open and watch for useful information and insights which will further equip you to lead the class session.

 Three things to note about the Session Plan:

One, the **Session Plan** makes heavy use of **Bible Learning Activities** (BLAs). A Bible Learning Activity is precisely what it sounds like—an activity students perform to learn about the Bible. Because action is employed, the student has a much greater chance of **comprehending** and **retaining** spiritual insights. And because you the leader can see what the student is doing—whether it's a written assignment, skit or art activity—you can readily **measure** the student's comprehension. The BLA allows you to **walk about the classroom** as students work, answering questions or dealing with problem students. Furthermore, it's **easier to teach well** using BLAs. If you've never used BLAs before, you will quickly find them much simpler to prepare and deliver than a whole session of lecture.

Two, the **Session Plan** provides guided conversation—suggestions on what to say throughout the class time. Notice that the guided conversation is always printed in **bold type** in the **Session Plan.** Regular light type indicates instructions to you, the teacher.

Three, if special or unusual preparation is required before class begins, it will be listed immediately below the title **SESSION PLAN,** under the heading **BEFORE CLASS BEGINS.**

3. SESSION PLAN

This heading introduces the step-by-step lesson plan. With careful planning, you can easily tailor each session to the amount of class time you have.

4. ATTENTION GRABBER

Who knows what lurks in the minds of your students as they file into your room? The **Attention Grabber** will stimulate their interest and focus their thinking on the theme of the lesson.

The **Attention Grabber,** as well as other parts of the **Session Plan,** often—but not always—contain an additional alternate activity. These alternates are identified by the titles **CREATIVE OPTION, OPTIONAL** or similar designations. Choose the activity that best suits the needs of your class and fits your time schedule.

5. BIBLE EXPLORATION

The **Bible Exploration** is the heart of your class session because it involves each learner directly in the study of God's Word. It is during this period that you will invite the students to explore and discover **what the Bible says and means** and to discuss **how it applies to each student.**

SESSION PLAN

BEFORE CLASS BEGINS: Photocopy enough Parchment worksheets for each student to l one. Locate a blueprint as described in the ATTENTION GRABBER.

Attention Grabber

ATTENTION GRABBER (3-5 minutes)

Materials needed: One or more blueprints or a draftsman's renderings of plans for a building. (These may be obtained from a contractor, architect or blueprint office. You can probably borrow some from your church office.)

When students are seated, show the blueprints and ask, **What are these for?** (They are a precise plan for building the structure.) Ask, **Why map out what the house is supposed to be?** (You need an exact plan in order to build it correctly and make sure you're going to get what you want.) **What would happen if you didn't use a blueprint?**

(The house would not be built correctly and migh be inconvenient or unsafe to live in.)

Make a transition to the next part of the sessio by saying something like this: **God has a bluepri for our lives. In order to have the kind of life that can withstand temptations and problem we must build by His plan. It's not enough just to know how the outside of our "house" should look; we must build according to plai in order to ensure that it turns out the right way. We do this by obediently following the rules God lays out.**

Bible Exploration

EXPLORATION (25-40 minutes)

Step 1 (3-5 minutes): Ask a volunteer to read Matthew 21:28-32. Drawing material from INSIGHTS FOR THE LEADER, give students a brief summary of the setting in which Jesus told this parable.

Step 2 (8-12 minutes): Have students get

together in groups of two or more. Tell them, **Take a close look at Matthew 21:28-30. Then retell the story as if it had happened to one of the groups of people listed on the Parchment worksheet.**

Step 3 (5-10 minutes): Reassemble class and asl

---

6. CONCLUSION AND DECISION

Each **Session Plan** provides this opportunity for students to deal with the questions, **What does the Bible mean to me? How can I put what I just learned into practice in my own life?** Be sure to leave enough time at the end of each session for the **Conclusion and Decision** activity.

7. NOTES

Every page of the **Session Plan** allows space for you to jot notes as you prepare for class. Also, you will find **important reminders** and **suggestions** listed in **bold type** to catch your attention.

● NECESSARY CLASSROOM SUPPLIES

The Session Plan Bible study activities require that you make the following items readily available to students:

- A Bible for each student (Essential!)   • Paper and pencils or pens
    - Felt markers   • Butcher paper for posters   • Transparent tape
        - Scissors

You, the teacher, will need a chalkboard and chalk, or overhead projector and transparencies.

Special requirements will be listed in the proper **Session Plans.**

THE PARCHMENT STUDENT WORKSHEETS

The **Parchment** helps students see the light of God's truth for themselves.

The page immediately following each **Session Plan** is the **Parchment** worksheet for your students. Here's how to use the **Parchment**, in 5 easy steps:

The
Parchment
SESSION 5

The Servant's Report

Read Luke 14:16-24. You are the servant asked to bring people to the feast. At the end of your day's work, fill out this report. Make sure to tell what happened and your feelings about it.

ACTIVITY LEDGER

Invitation List

Perhaps you know some friends or relatives who need to be invited to know Christ. List them below.

PEOPLE TO INVITE TO THE HEAVENLY BANQUET

● TRY THESE SPECIAL TIPS:

Photocopy all youth group announcements on the reverse side of the **Parchment.** The **Clip Art and Other Goodies** section at the back of this book will be a big help here.

Use different colored paper from week to week in your copier. If your machine can enlarge, print the worksheets "giant size" once in awhile.

Too much of even a good thing is too much. We suggest that every now and then you hand out blank paper and simply *read* the **Parchment** instructions to your students. Or write the instructions on the chalkboard. Or hand write and copy your own worksheets. Variety is the key.

1. Before class, use your church photocopier to reproduce enough student worksheets for your learners and a few extra for visitors. There is rarely more than one **PARCHMENT** worksheet per session—one session (#3) has none at all.

2. The **Parchments** are generally used throughout each **Session Plan.** The best time to distribute them to students is when the **Session Plan** first calls for their use. Always keep a copy for yourself.

3. Be sure to have plenty of blank paper for students' written assignments— the **Parchments** don't have much extra space.

4. It may help to have your students fold their **Parchment** into their Bibles if there is a gap between uses of the worksheet. This will aid you in avoiding the Paper Airplane Syndrome.

5. Collect and save the worksheets occasionally. (Do not collect worksheets that contain private confessions to God or the like.) You can follow the progress of your students by examining their work. Parents, too, will want to see what their kids are learning.

THE TEACHING RESOURCE PAGES

Special goodies to help you teach.

A few sessions require extra goodies such as board games or short stories. These are provided by the **Teaching Resource** pages which follow the **Parchment** student worksheet in the appropriate sessions.

The **Session Plans** and the **Teaching Resource** pages contain complete instructions.

Teaching Resource 4 **Instructions: Cut apart all the slips on this page (if you expect more than twelve students in your class, make enough photocopies of this page for each student to have one slip.)**

Solve this riddle: "Part of the time I come for free, the rest of the time you pay for me. What am I?"	**Solve this riddle:** "I am faster than the fastest thing, but if I run into you, you'll feel no sting. What am I?"	**Solve this riddle:** "Here's a tough one— I come in waves, but I'm not the ocean. What am I?"
Solve this riddle: "Part of the time I come for free, the rest of the time you pay for me. What am I?"	**Solve this riddle:** "I am faster than the fastest thing, but if I run into you, you'll feel no sting. What am I?"	**Solve this riddle:** "Here's a tough one— I come in waves, but I'm not the ocean. What am I?"
Solve this riddle: "Part of the time I come for free, the rest of the time you pay for me. What am I?"	**Solve this riddle:** "I am faster than the fastest thing, but if I run into you, you'll feel no sting. What am I?"	**Solve this riddle:** "Here's a tough one— I come in waves, but I'm not the ocean. What am I?"
Solve this riddle: "Part of the time I come for free, the rest of the time you pay for me. What am I?"	**Solve this riddle:** "I am faster than the fastest thing, but if I run into you, you'll feel no sting. What am I?"	**Solve this riddle:** "Here's a tough one— I come in waves, but I'm not the ocean. What am I?"

THE FUN PAGE TAKE-HOME PAPERS

Give your students a treat! The Fun Page combines games, memory verses and daily devotional studies into an enjoyable, fun-filled take-home paper.

Features:

Each **Fun Page** contains a Bible game designed to amplify the insights gained in the classroom. Mazes, crosswords, word searches—games ranging from the simple to the extremely challenging.

There's cartoon artwork, informal readability, and humor that your students will welcome.

The **Daily Nuggets** section is a simple six-day devotional based on passages related to the Scriptures studied in class. See "TIPS" on the next page for important advice.

The **Hot Thot** memory verse helps students lock the wisdom of God's Word into their minds and hearts.

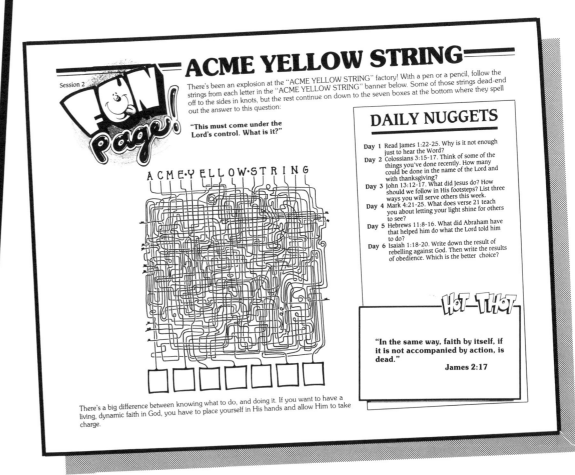

ACME YELLOW STRING

Session 2

There's been an explosion at the "ACME YELLOW STRING" factory! With a pen or a pencil, follow the strings from each letter in the "ACME YELLOW STRING" banner below. Some of those strings dead-end off to the sides in knots, but the rest continue on down to the seven boxes at the bottom where they spell out the answer to this question:

"This must come under the Lord's control. What is it?"

A C M E · Y E L L O W · S T R I N G

DAILY NUGGETS

Day 1 Read James 1:22-25. Why is it not enough just to hear the Word?

Day 2 Colossians 3:15-17. Think of some of the things you've done recently. How many could be done in the name of the Lord and with thanksgiving?

Day 3 John 13:12-17. What did Jesus do? How should we follow in His footsteps? List three ways you will serve others this week.

Day 4 Mark 4:21-25. What does verse 21 teach you about letting your light shine for others to see?

Day 5 Hebrews 11:8-16. What did Abraham have that helped him do what the Lord told him to do?

Day 6 Isaiah 1:18-20. Write down the result of rebelling against God. Then write the results of obedience. Which is the better choice?

HoT THoT

"In the same way, faith by itself, if it is not accompanied by action, is dead."

James 2:17

There's a big difference between knowing what to do, and doing it. If you want to have a living, dynamic faith in God, you have to place yourself in His hands and allow Him to take charge.

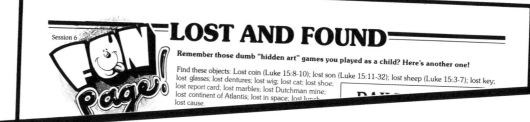

LOST AND FOUND

Remember those dumb "hidden art" games you played as a child? Here's another one!

Find these objects: Lost coin (Luke 15:8-10); lost son (Luke 15:11-32); lost sheep (Luke 15:3-7); lost key; lost glasses; lost dentures; lost wig; lost cat; lost shoe; lost report card; lost marbles; lost Dutchman mine; lost continent of Atlantis; lost in space; lost lunch; lost cause.

TIPS:

You can use the Fun Page several ways:

As a **take-home paper** to extend the classroom into the week. Hand out copies as students leave class.

As a special **Bible Learning Activity** during class. (Some of the games would make interesting **Attention Grabbers,** for example.)

Make it the **focal point of another Bible study.** For instance, if you used the **Session Plan** Sunday morning, you could reinforce the lesson during an informal midweek meeting by involving students in answering the questions in the **Daily Nuggets** section.

Even absentees can be involved. Put the **Fun Page** into an envelope along with a personal note to that learner who needs a little encouragement.

A word about MOTIVATION:

You won't have any trouble getting your students to play the games on the **Fun Page.** (Just see how many of them are playing the games during church service!) But the **Daily Nuggets** and the **Hot Thot** memory verse can be problems. Here are two ways to motivate students to answer the daily devotional questions and memorize the verse:

1. Start a contest. Award points to those students who complete the assignments, bring friends and memorize passages. Pick a nice prize such as a free trip to camp and run the contest for about five weeks. (Longer makes for lack of interest.)

2. Combine the assignments with a discipleship class. If you are not personally involved in the discipleship program, give a copy of the **Fun Page** to the leader.

THE POPSHEET LECTURE BIBLE STUDIES

"Pop" these Popsheets out of this book and give them to the leader of your youth group's other meetings. Great for an at- home Bible study, a camp retreat, games night or special event.

Youth groups come in all sizes and shapes. So do youth programs. Meetings vary widely in style—ranging from Sunday morning Bible studies with singing and announcements, to deeper discipleship programs for motivated students, to the fun and action of game nights with very short Bible messages.

The **Popsheets** offer a good source of creative thinking for whatever type of program you have. **Popsheets** are packed with Bible stories, object lessons, case studies, discussion questions and fast-paced games aimed at the junior high "squirrel" mentality! Each **Popsheet** covers the same basic theme as the accompanying **Session Plan,** but the stories, verses, object lessons and case studies are all new and fresh. The advantages?

- For students who attended the **Session Plan** class, a fresh new perspective on the topic. A great way to insure retention.

- For learners who missed the **Session Plan** class, a good way to keep current with the other students. This is a sound method to guarantee that all your youth group members explore every topic in a Bible study series.

- Or use your creativity to replace some of the Bible Learning Activities in the **Session Plan** with the **Popsheets'** object lessons and short stories.

THEME

Roughly the same theme as the accompanying **Session Plan.**

BIBLE STUDY OUTLINE

A suggested Bible passage with a list of important points to make during your lecture, the **Bible Study Outline** offers a **basic** lesson plan to stimulate your thinking as you prayerfully prepare your message. **Use your own creativity and ability to "flesh it out."** There is plenty here for outstanding Bible messages your students will enjoy and remember.

Notice that the **Bible Study Outline** contains no **Bible Learning Activities.** The **Popsheet** is designed to be a short Bible message that you can give at an informal games night, camp cabin devotional, or what have you.

OBJECT LESSON

Each **Popsheet** has an object lesson, short story or case study. (A case study is a description of an event or situation a junior high student is likely to face in life.) These add spice to your messages. A good object lesson, for instance, and the spiritual truth it conveys, can be remembered for a lifetime.

DISCUSSION QUESTIONS

You may wish to involve your students in your lectures by asking them about the issues and implications of the Bible study. Feel free to modify or add to the questions to more nearly suit your students' needs.

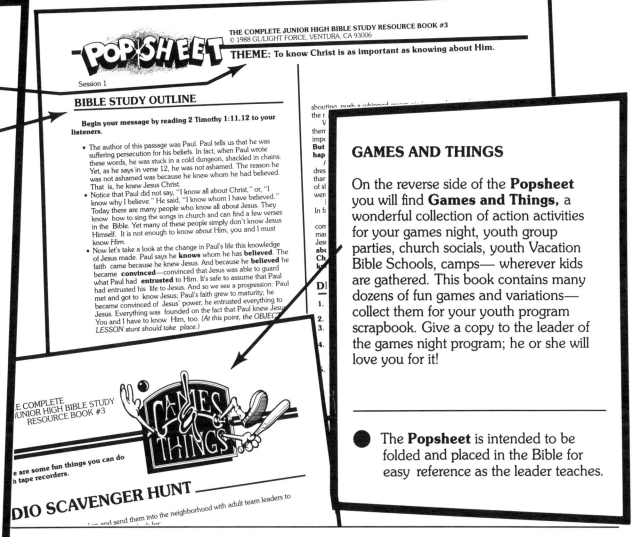

THE COMPLETE JUNIOR HIGH BIBLE STUDY RESOURCE BOOK #3
© 1988 GL/LIGHT FORCE, VENTURA, CA 93006

THEME: To know Christ is as important as knowing about Him.

Session 1

BIBLE STUDY OUTLINE

Begin your message by reading 2 Timothy 1:11,12 to your listeners.

- The author of this passage was Paul. Paul tells us that he was suffering persecution for his beliefs. In fact, when Paul wrote these words, he was stuck in a cold dungeon, shackled in chains. Yet, as he says in verse 12, he was not ashamed. The reason he was not ashamed was because he knew whom he had believed. That is, he knew Jesus Christ.
- Notice that Paul did not say, "I know all about Christ," or, "I know why I believe." He said, "I know whom I have believed." Today there are many people who know all *about* Jesus. They know how to sing the songs in church and can find a few verses in the Bible. Yet many of these people simply don't know Jesus Himself. It is not enough to know *about* Him, you and I must know *Him.*
- Now let's take a look at the change in Paul's life this knowledge of Jesus made. Paul says he **knows** whom he has **believed.** The faith came because he knew Jesus. And because he **believed** he became **convinced**—convinced that Jesus was able to guard what Paul had **entrusted** to Him. It's safe to assume that Paul had entrusted his life to Jesus. And so we see a progression: Paul met and got to know Jesus; Paul's faith grew to maturity; he became convinced of Jesus' power; he entrusted everything to Jesus. Everything was founded on the fact that Paul knew Jesus. You and I have to know Him, too. *(At this point, the OBJECT LESSON stunt should take place.)*

GAMES AND THINGS

On the reverse side of the **Popsheet** you will find **Games and Things,** a wonderful collection of action activities for your games night, youth group parties, church socials, youth Vacation Bible Schools, camps— wherever kids are gathered. This book contains many dozens of fun games and variations— collect them for your youth program scrapbook. Give a copy to the leader of the games night program; he or she will love you for it!

● The **Popsheet** is intended to be folded and placed in the Bible for easy reference as the leader teaches.

The **Popsheet** is an exciting addition to the LIGHT FORCE line of junior high Bible study materials. It contains truly useful features that will help make your informal Bible study meetings of keen interest to your learners.

The **Popsheet** is for you to use. Take advantage of it. Use it as an aid to your Bible study preparation and game plans. You'll be glad you did.

INTRODUCTION TO CLIP ART

Good news for those who can't draw.

If you want your class or youth group to increase in size—and who doesn't—you'll welcome the **Clip Art and Other Goodies** section found at the rear of this book. Create your own terrific monthly youth group activity calendars, announcement sheets and posters. It's fun and easy! Simply follow the tips and techniques in the **Clip Art and Other Goodies** section; you'll produce great "promo pieces" that will attract kids to your Bible studies and other events.

Remember: Even if you can't draw cartoons, with the right promotional clip art you can draw kids!

CLIP ART AND OTHER GOODIES

The following pages contain all sorts of fun, high quality clip art. Put it to good use: brighten up your youth group's mail outs, bulletins, posters and overhead transparencies. Cut 'em out, paste 'em up, run 'em off and there you have it!

You'll be happy to know that the LIGHT FORCE publishes two great clip art books for youth workers: the original YOUTH WORKER'S CLIP ART BOOK and the famous SON OF CLIP ART! Available at your local Christian supply store, or write

THE LIGHT FORCE
P.O. BOX 6309
OXNARD, CA 93031

WANT TO PRODUCE GREAT PROMOTIONAL MATERIAL? TURN THE PAGE FOR EASY INSTRUCTIONS . . .

157

The House on the Rock

INSIGHTS FOR THE LEADER

WHAT THE SESSION IS ABOUT

Choosing a foundation for life.

SCRIPTURE STUDIED

Matthew 7:24-27; 1 Corinthians 3:11-14.

KEY PASSAGE

"Therefore everyone who hears these words of mine and puts them into practice is like a wise man who built his house on the rock."
Matthew 7:24

AIMS OF THE SESSION

During this session your learners will:

1. Identify the results of choices in selecting life's foundations;
2. Tell what each symbol in Christ's parable means to us today;
3. Acknowledge their personal choices of foundations.

This is background material for you, the teacher, to use as you prepare to guide your students through this Bible study session. It should give you sufficient material to guide discussions as indicated in the SESSION PLAN which follows.

With this session you are beginning a new course in which you and your class will be studying the parables of Jesus. Our Lord did much of His teaching in the form of parables, which have been called "earthly stories with heavenly meanings." Jesus used parables to gain and hold the interest of those who heard Him. His listeners were quite familiar with the earthly settings of His parables. Jesus used the familiar to present an important spiritual lesson. In order to understand a parable you and your students will need to see its major point, or theme.

The parable for this session is concerned with the choices people make about the foundation on which they build their lives. Over the next several weeks you and your students will study how a life may be built on Jesus Christ.

The Foundations

This week's parable concerns two men, each with a common need to build a home (see Matt. 7:24-27). The wise man chose to build his house on a solid foundation, the rock. The foolish man chose to build on sand, a loose foundation. Each man's house was tested by storm. The home on the faulty foundation was destroyed; the home on the rock was preserved. The preservation or destruction of the respective houses was determined by the choice of location. Good materials and craftsmanship might have gone into both houses, but the deciding factor in destruction or preservation was the locations the builders chose for their houses.

The only safe foundation is Jesus. In this parable Jesus pictures two builders, each needing a house. The houses represent their individual lives. The wise one builds upon a rock. The foolish one builds in the sand. There is always a temptation to build upon the sand. This is especially true in Palestine, where much of the land is hilly and rocky. It is difficult to level the ground and set the foundation in rock. During the long summer months the river and creek beds are bone dry. In these low places there are flat stretches of sand, easy to level and easy to build upon. It is an inviting place. It requires no hard work; it is the easy way.

When Jesus spoke of sand, He meant any philosophy, life-style or value system not patterned on His teaching. Your students are at a point of observing and possibly experimenting with various faulty foundations for life. Some will be strongly inclined to build or center their lives on sports, popularity, sex or material things. These interests, like sand, are inviting

NOTES

and seem to offer an easy life.

But the builder who selects the sandy place is shortsighted. He has not considered the future. As long as summer remains, there is no real danger. But summer must turn to fall. With the first storm that flat, low, sandy spot is deluged with torrents of brown water. The place of ease and safety is overwhelmed by raging water. The house placed in such a location cannot survive. It will be destroyed.

The Storms

The destruction comes because of a storm. Rain and winds and storms come into our lives. Your students may be encountering some storms. They may be caught in tension between themselves and their parents. They may be under severe peer pressure to be liked and accepted. They may be seeing their illusions of romance, team victory or stardom dissolving before their eyes. They may be weathering the storm of divorce or death in the family. At times like these the foundation of their lives is tested.

Every person must have a foundation for life; every life will be tested by some sort of storm. We have a choice between rock and sand. The person who builds on the rock is the person who hears and practices the word of Jesus.

In the Greek language there are two words which speak of rock. These words are *petros* and *petra*. Petros is a rock formation like a mountain or cliff. Petra is a piece of rock or boulder. In this parable Jesus spoke of the petros, a great rock formation. We build on the great rock foundation by hearing and doing what Jesus taught.

The Rock

That petros, the huge foundation rock, is Jesus Christ, the Son of the living God. Jesus identifies Himself as the only sure foundation upon which we can build our lives. Jesus is the only foundation great enough to withstand the rains, wind and storms of life. He is the rock that no storm can overcome. He is the rock who gives us security. Through this parable Jesus showed that we have the choice to found our lives upon the rock, Jesus Christ, or to build our lives on sand, and lose everything. The wise person builds his or her house on the rock—Jesus!

The Building

After exploring the meaning of this parable, students will also examine 1 Corinthians 3:11-14, which describes Jesus as the foundation and then lists various materials with which one might build a structure upon that foundation. These are gold, silver, costly stones, wood, hay or straw. These building materials will be tested by fire. The gold, silver and costly stones (which may represent marble and other types of stone used for building) will survive, but the wood, hay and straw will be destroyed.

This analogy speaks of the importance of building with lasting materials upon the foundation. The precious materials represent values, attitudes and actions that build up the person's relationship with Christ and with other people. The flammable materials represent values, attitudes and actions that are destructive to the person and to those around him or her.

With Jesus Christ as the foundation, and with lasting values, attitudes and actions as building materials, your students can build lives that honor God and produce results that will last into eternity.

SESSION PLAN

BEFORE CLASS BEGINS: Photocopy enough Parchment worksheets for each student to have one. Obtain real estate ads as described in the EXPLORATION.

Attention Grabber

ATTENTION GRABBER (5 minutes)

Before class, letter the following questions on newsprint: 1. What would be the most dangerous place to build a house? Why? 2. What would be the safest place to build a house?

Post the newsprint on a wall of your classroom where all may see.

Have students form groups of two or more. Instruct them, **In your groups you are to discuss the questions posted on the wall. Arrive at a majority opinion about each question and be prepared to share that opinion with the rest of us.**

After allowing 2 minutes for group discussion, call the class to order and let a representative of each group report the group's opinions.

Make a transition to the EXPLORATION by saying something like this: **You've pointed out some obviously dangerous places to build a house. I know that none of you would be so foolish as to buy or build a house in any of these places. Although people are usually careful about where they put their houses, many are careless about the base upon which they build their lives. Jesus told an**

interesting story about this very kind of person.

Explain that today's session deals with a parable of Christ's in which He used the idea of building a house to teach about building a life.

CREATIVE ALTERNATE (5 minutes)

Materials needed: Several bricks, a bag or bucket of sand.

Show your students the bricks and sand (pour the sand onto a sheet of butcher paper on the desk or floor). Ask a volunteer to come forward and build a tower by stacking the bricks. Now ask another student to build a tower with the sand.

Make a transition to the EXPLORATION by saying something like, **Obviously, only a fool would attempt to build a real structure with loose sand—it can't be done. But today we are going to take a look at a story Jesus told about this very kind of fool.**

Explain that today's session deals with a parable of Christ's in which He used the idea of building a house to teach about building a life.

15

NOTES

Bible Exploration

EXPLORATION (25-40 minutes)

Materials needed: Several sample real estate ads from your local paper or, better still, a few copies of real estate magazines that can usually be obtained for free at banks and real estate offices.

Step 1 (5-8 minutes): Read Matthew 7:24-27 to your students (or ask volunteers to read). Then direct students' attention to The Parchment worksheet. Discuss the questions in the "What Does It Represent?" section. Add additional information as needed, using material from INSIGHTS FOR THE LEADER.

Step 2 (10-15 minutes): Show the sample real estate ads you have brought, and post them on the wall where students can see them. Assemble students into small groups. Provide paper and felt pens. Explain, **You're going to design a real estate ad that tells about the advantages of building your life on the foundation of Jesus Christ, and the foolishness of buying a house built on sand (the world's values). Your ad should be worded in a way that shows that the solid foundation is Christ and the sand foundation is the world, or things or values that are faulty. For example, you might call the structures built on a sand foundation "Popularity Shores Condominiums" or "Materialism Valley Development." Add illustrations to your ad.**

Step 3 (3-5 minutes): Regain the attention of the class and ask volunteers to show their ads. Thank those who participate.

Step 4 (5-7 minutes): Comment, **We have discussed some foundations upon which people tend to build their lives. Now we're going to look at the construction materials that can be used to build a solid structure for our lives. Return to your groups and look at the "A.C.M.E. Building Supply Sheet" section of your Parchment worksheet. Read 1 Corinthians 3:11-14 and answer the questions on the worksheet.**

Step 5 (3-5 minutes): Reassemble the class and have groups report their responses. Point out, **Gold, silver and precious stones would survive a fire, while wood, hay and straw would be destroyed. The former are the worthwhile materials with which to build a life; the latter are the valueless elements. The worthwhile building materials are values, attitudes and actions that promote your growth in Christ and your relationships with people around you. The worthless elements are values, attitudes and actions that are destructive to yourself and to others. It's important to evaluate the kind of lives we are building on the foundation of Jesus Christ.** Ask, **What would happen to a life built of gold, silver and precious stones that was constructed on sand? Obviously, God wants us to have both a solid foundation and quality materials in our lives.**

Conclusion and Decision

CONCLUSION (2-3 minutes)

Have students turn to the worksheet section titled, "Which House Is You?" Explain, **Today would be a good time to stop and check the values that we are building our lives on. We either have Christ as our foundation or we don't. I want you to look at the pictures for a few moments and decide which of these houses represents you right now. There is also a place to check if you want to start building your house on Jesus, the Rock, right now. You won't be asked to show your answers to anyone; but if you'd like some help in beginning to build your house on the Rock, I'd be happy to talk with you after class.** Allow 1 minute for students to complete the assignment.

Close in prayer and distribute the Fun Page take-home paper.

Your students may wish to see these solutions to the Fun Page Puzzle.

(If you like, write one or both solutions on an extra copy of the Fun Page and pin it to your classroom bulletin board.)

SAND	**SAND**
SANK	**SANK**
RANK	**SACK**
RACK	**SOCK**
ROCK	**ROCK**

(There may be other solutions.)

Note: Locate a blueprint to use in the next session (see page 27 for details).

SESSION 1

What Does It Represent?

From the story you've just read in Matthew 7:24-27, what do you think the items in the story symbolize?

● **Rising Streams (floods)** ● **Rock**

● **Rain** ● **Wind** ● **Sand** ● **House**

What do you think caused each builder to build his house where he did?

●A.C.M.E. Building● Supply Sheet

A.C.M.E. = All Christlike Materials Engineering

Read 1 Corinthians 3:11-14 and then fill out the answers to the following questions:

1. What foundation is mentioned in this passage?

2. In case of fire, which of the following building materials would catch on fire?

☐ Gold   ☐ Wood   ☐ Costly stones

☐ Silver   ☐ Hay   ☐ Straw

3. The building materials represent values and attitudes that a person might have and actions a person might do. List some specific values, attitudes and actions that are good and would tend to cause a Christian to grow in the Lord, and then list some that are harmful or worthless.

Which House Is You?

Check the box next to the house that represents you.

Built on Jesus: the Solid Rock

WOOD, HAY STRAW   ½ WOOD, ½ GOLD   GOLD, SILVER, PRECIOUS STONES

Built on self: a sandy foundation

☐ I'd like to build my house on the rock starting now!

☐ I need help building my house with the right values.

FUN Page!

Session 1

SAND TO ROCK

If you've read Matthew 7:24-27, you know that Jesus compared the wise person who listens to His words to a wise man who built a house on rock. And He said that the one who ignores His words is like a man who builds on sand—a fool. The house on the rock withstands storms; the house on the sand washes away. Jesus' point was that we should build our lives on His words. If you're afraid you have been building on sand, you probably want to know how to change over to the rock. This fun brain teaser will help you answer the question, "How do you change sand to rock?"

Instructions: The object of this puzzler is to change the word *sand* to the word *rock*. You do this by changing one letter at a time, each time forming a new word—a real word (see our example).

Example: **SAND**
          SEND
          REND
          RIND
          RINK
          RICK
          ROCK

This is a lousy example because it contains a proper name (Rick) and because it's pretty long. We found a shorter way to do it that takes only three new words. Can you find it? Fill in the blanks below to find the proper words. If you can't find the solution, ask the person who gave you this paper. (There is more than one solution.)

SAND _____

_____

_____ **ROCK**

Now that you've played the game: Of course, if you want to get your life rebuilt on Christ the Solid Rock instead of shifting sands, you have to do a bit more than solve a brain teaser. You must commit yourself to Christ, regular Bible study, prayer, making friends with other Christians, and beginning a new style of living (obedience to Jesus). If you do these things, your life will be strong because Jesus is strong. He'll make sure you get through the storms of life.

DAILY NUGGETS Wisdom from God's Word for you to read each day.

Day 1 Read Luke 6:46-49. Which foundation would you rather build on?

Day 2 Matthew 7:24-27. Name two things Jesus asked you to do that you are now doing.

Day 3 1 Corinthians 3:10,11. Who is our only foundation? What sort of life are you building on this foundation?

Day 4 Ephesians 2:19-22. As members of God's household, we have Christ as our cornerstone. Explain what happens to Christians according to verse 22.

Day 5 Isaiah 28:16. Who is the stone God is laying in Zion?

Day 6 Psalm 18:2. Write Psalm 18:2 on an index card and place it where you will see it first thing in the morning. Read it each day until you have it memorized.

Hot Thot

"Therefore everyone who hears these words of mine and puts them into practice is like a wise man who built his house on the rock."
Matthew 7:24

THEME: To know Christ is as important as knowing about Him.

Session 1

BIBLE STUDY OUTLINE

Begin your message by reading 2 Timothy 1:11,12 to your listeners.

- The author of this passage was Paul. Paul tells us that he was suffering persecution for his beliefs. In fact, when Paul wrote these words, he was stuck in a cold dungeon, shackled in chains. Yet, as he says in verse 12, he was not ashamed. The reason he was not ashamed was because he knew whom he had believed. That is, he knew Jesus Christ.
- Notice that Paul did not say, "I know all about Christ," or, "I know why I believe." He said, "I know whom I have believed." Today there are many people who know all *about* Jesus. They know how to sing the songs in church and can find a few verses in the Bible. Yet many of these people simply don't know Jesus Himself. It is not enough to know *about* Him, you and I must know *Him*.
- Now let's take a look at the change in Paul's life this knowledge of Jesus made. Paul says he **knows** whom he has **believed**. The faith came because he knew Jesus. And because he **believed** he became **convinced**—convinced that Jesus was able to guard what Paul had **entrusted** to Him. It's safe to assume that Paul had entrusted his life to Jesus. And so we see a progression: Paul met and got to know Jesus; Paul's faith grew to maturity; he became convinced of Jesus' power; he entrusted everything to Jesus. Everything was founded on the fact that Paul knew Jesus. You and I have to know Him, too. (*At this point, the OBJECT LESSON stunt should take place.*)

OBJECT LESSON:
WHAT DO YOU KNOW?

Have an adult (a stranger to your students or someone in a disguise) sneak unnoticed into the room, suddenly run up to you while shouting, push a whipped cream pie in your face and quickly run out of the room.

Wipe your face off with a towel and calm students down. Reassure them that the act was planned by you as a demonstration of an important point. Say something like, **You all saw what happened. But how many of you can accurately recall details of what just happened? Let's find out.**

Ask questions like these: What color was the person's pants (skirt, dress)? Was he or she wearing a watch? Was the person taller or shorter than me? How many seconds was the person in the room? What kind of shoes did the person wear? Which door did he or she come in? What were his or her exact words?

Probably no single person will have the answers to all the questions. In fact, some questions may stump the whole group.

Point out that, just like the students who really don't have a completely accurate knowledge of the details of this amazing incident, many Christians really don't have a clear or complete knowledge of Jesus Christ. Say, **Too many Christians just learn a few basics about Christ, but never seem to get to know *Him*. Paul knew Christ. That was the most important thing to him. And knowing Jesus should be the most important thing to us.**

DISCUSSION QUESTIONS

1. **What's the difference between knowing about Christ and knowing Christ?**
2. **How can Christians get to know Him better?**
3. **Will there ever be a point when we can say we know Him perfectly? Why or why not?**
4. **Paul says he believed, was convinced and had entrusted himself to Jesus. What do all these words mean? How can they be experienced in our own lives today?**
5. **Paul says he entrusted to Him for "that day." What day do you suppose that is? Is that day important to us? What happens to the person who is not prepared for that day?**

THE COMPLETE
JUNIOR HIGH BIBLE STUDY
RESOURCE BOOK #3

Here are some fun things you can do with tape recorders.

AUDIO SCAVENGER HUNT

Provide teams with cassette recorders and send them into the neighborhood with adult team leaders to collect sounds. Here are some suggestions of what to look for:

A man's voice singing a verse from "I Did It My Way."
The squeal of air being released from a balloon.
A gas station bell.
The sound of a cash register.
A cat's meow (or a woman imitating a cat).
A dog's bark.
Water running in a sink or bathtub.
A television commercial for food.
"Welcome to MacDonald's. May I take your order please?" (Said over the drive-up intercom.)
A piano or electric guitar.

NAME THAT TUNE

Borrow all the record albums you can find (from "goldies" to current) and create several minutes worth of quick clips from the better-known songs. Each clip should be two to three seconds long. Play the first clip to your group. The first person to recognize the song jumps up and is allowed to make his or her guess. A right guess scores five points; a wrong guess loses one point. Keep track of the scores.

NAME THAT SOUND

The same as "NAME THAT TUNE," except players are to guess the source of sounds you've recorded. In addition to some of the sounds listed in "AUDIO SCAVENGER HUNT," try:

A washing machine.
The engine of a car.
A skateboard.
The splash of someone diving into a pool.
A dog with long toenails walking on a tile floor.
A chair being shoved backward on a tile floor.

Building by the Plans

Session 2

INSIGHTS FOR THE LEADER

WHAT THE SESSION IS ABOUT

We build our Christian lives by obedience to Christ.

SCRIPTURE STUDIED

Matthew 21:28-32; James 2:14-18.

KEY PASSAGE

"In the same way, faith by itself, if it is not accompanied by action, is dead." James 2:17

AIMS OF THE SESSION

During this session your learners will:

1. Identify obedience as a main ingredient for building one's life in Christ;
2. Describe specific areas in which Christians should be obedient;
3. Select an area of obedience to put into action.

God wants us to do what He asks. This is the thrust of the parable of the two sons which your class will be studying in this session. The parables of Jesus are just as relevant today as they were when He gave them. Boys haven't changed much! They are still having problems doing what their parents ask them to do.

This parable is the result of the questioning of Jesus' authority. Jesus had entered the city as a royal monarch. The people had lined the streets of Jerusalem blessing Him and shouting "Hosanna to the Son of David" (Matt. 21:9). He entered the Temple and, as the Lord of the Temple, He drove out those who were making it a street market " 'It is written', he said to them, 'My house will be called a house of prayer,' but you are making it a 'den of robbers' " (verse 13).

By this action Jesus was claiming to be the very "Lord of the Temple." Of course the religious establishment was not going to take that lying down. They challenged the claims that He made for Himself (both overt and implied), especially that of messiahship. Because of His popularity they could not arrest Him for His actions. They hoped that they could catch Him by His own words—that He would blaspheme God and thus they could stone Him to death. So, with subtle skill, they questioned Him. " 'By what authority are you doing these things?' they asked. 'And who gave you this authority?' " (verse 23). In response, Jesus

posed a question for them to answer: "John's baptism—where did it come from? Was it from heaven, or from men?" (verse 25). They could not answer, because to say "from heaven" would have given credence to John's attacks on them (see Matt. 3:7) and to say "from men" would have placed them in disfavor with the crowds.

Following this exchange, Jesus answered their question in a very clever way. He spoke of a father with two sons. The father asked his sons to go to the vineyard to work. The first son refused to go, but later changed his mind and did what his father had asked. The second son politely responded, " 'I will, sir,' but he did not go" (Matt. 21:30).

The first son represents the tax collectors and base sinners of Jesus' day. Their lives were a denial of having anything at all to do with God. They denied God most rudely by their words and deeds. Some students may have done the same by denying Jesus in their lives. Thus, they are like the first son.

However, at the preaching of John the Baptist and Jesus Christ, the tax collectors and sinners changed their minds. They repented. They realized that their lives were going in the wrong direction and they turned them around. It is this change of direction that God was and is looking for. It is not enough to recognize error or even feel guilty about it. One must turn from it to qualify for repentance. By their

actions they became obedient to God the Father. Jesus said to the Jewish leaders, "I tell you the truth, the tax collectors and the prostitutes are entering the kingdom of God ahead of you" (verse 31).

The second son represents those who claimed to serve God. Yet their profession did not agree with their practice. They claimed godliness but didn't live godliness. Despite the preaching of John the Baptist and Jesus Christ, they would not repent; they would not change. Ultimately, in their disobedience, they brought about the execution of Jesus.

The priests and elders to whom Jesus was speaking recognized the first son as preferable, evidently failing to see themselves as the second son until Jesus pointed this out to them.

Of course Jesus Himself is the perfect Son. He obeyed His Father right from the start. The religious leaders had asked Him, "By what authority are you doing these things?" (verse 23). They wanted to know how He could receive the praise of the people and claim to be the Lord of the Temple. Jesus' response indicated that His authority to do what He did is based upon His relationship to God, His Father. He is the Son of God and He came to do the will of His Father. A true son is one who does the Father's will. His Father's will was that He would come to the Father's vineyard to bring in a harvest. You and your class are part of that harvest. The harvest is brought in by our faith and obedience to Jesus. Jesus has said, "If anyone loves me, he will obey my teaching. My Father will love him, and we will come to him and make our home with him" (John 14:23). Jesus' words are clear. If we are to be His, we must obey Him!

And what is His command that we are to obey? He said that the great commandment is, " 'Love the Lord your God with all your heart and with all your soul and with all your mind and with all your strength.' The second is this: 'Love your neighbor as yourself.' There is no commandment greater than these" (Mark 12:30,31).

Love God and love other people—these are the two basic commands our Lord expects us to obey. Our relationship with Jesus is not isolated from the rest of life. If we belong to Him, He expects us to obey Him by loving other people.

James spoke to this issue when he wrote, "What good is it, my brothers, if a man claims to have faith but has no deeds? Can such faith save him? Suppose a brother or sister is without clothes and daily food. If one of you says to him, 'Go, I wish you well; keep warm and well fed,' but does nothing about his physical needs, what good is it? In the same way, faith by itself, if it is not accompanied by action, is dead. But someone will say, 'You have faith; I have deeds.' Show me your faith without deeds, and I will show you my faith by what I do" (Jas. 2:14-18).

Jesus gives us a principle to live by in this parable. True faith results in action. That action generally works itself out in attitudes and behavior towards other people.

At home, at school and just "messing around," your students will have the opportunity to obey God by setting their priorities in line with His teachings as found in Scripture. The results will be a surprising difference in the way they deal with their friends, family and enemies.

SESSION PLAN

BEFORE CLASS BEGINS: Photocopy enough Parchment worksheets for each student to have one. Locate a blueprint as described in the ATTENTION GRABBER.

Attention Grabber

ATTENTION GRABBER (3-5 minutes)

Materials needed: One or more blueprints or a draftsman's renderings of plans for a building. (These may be obtained from a contractor, architect or blueprint office. You can probably borrow some from your church office.)

When students are seated, show the blueprints and ask, **What are these for?** (They are a precise plan for building the structure.) Ask, **Why map out what the house is supposed to be?** (You need an exact plan in order to build it correctly and make sure you're going to get what you want.) **What would happen if you didn't use a blueprint?**

(The house would not be built correctly and might be inconvenient or unsafe to live in.)

Make a transition to the next part of the session by saying something like this: **God has a blueprint for our lives. In order to have the kind of life that can withstand temptations and problems we must build by His plan. It's not enough just to know how the outside of our "house" should look; we must build according to plan in order to ensure that it turns out the right way. We do this by obediently following the rules God lays out.**

Bible Exploration

EXPLORATION (25-40 minutes)

Step 1 (3-5 minutes): Ask a volunteer to read Matthew 21:28-32. Drawing material from INSIGHTS FOR THE LEADER, give students a brief summary of the setting in which Jesus told this parable.

Step 2 (8-12 minutes): Have students get

together in groups of two or more. Tell them, **Take a close look at Matthew 21:28-30. Then retell the story as if it had happened to one of the groups of people listed on the Parchment worksheet.**

Step 3 (5-10 minutes): Reassemble class and ask

NOTES

for a few volunteers to share their stories. Make sure they understand the basic "plot" of the parable (not the interpretation—that comes next).

Step 4 (5-7 minutes): Now lead a discussion with the entire class based on verses 31 and 32. Ask, **Why was the first son considered better than the second son?** (God values action, not talk.) **To what group did Jesus compare the first son?** (Tax collectors and prostitutes.) **To what group did Jesus compare the second son?** (Chief priests and elders.) **What would have happened if the first son felt guilty about not helping his father but still did not go to work for him?** (He would not have entered the Kingdom of God.) **What does the story tell you about what repentance really is?** (Turning from disobedience and starting to do what God wants us to do.)

Step 5 (5-7 minutes): Instruct students, **In today's parable Jesus raised the issue of people who claim to serve God, but whose lives don't match their claims. Let's look at another section of the Bible that goes a little deeper into this problem.** Read James 2:14-18 aloud while the rest follow in their own Bibles.

Write the following words on chalkboard or flipchart for all to see: Home, Others, Self. Tell students, **The Scripture we have just read shows us how our obedience to Christ will have an effect on other areas of our lives. The example was caring for another person's physical needs, but the principle applies to every area of our lives. Let's think of several ways our obedience to Christ affects the areas I've written on the board: home, others and ourselves.**

Ideas might include: Home—do what parents ask without griping; be considerate of others' property; treat family members with courtesy; Others—Forgive; love enemies; don't gossip; tell people about Christ; Self—avoid drugs and alcohol; control sexual urges; maintain physical fitness; eat right.

As groups work, you may need to prod some of your students with questions or comments such as these: **If you and Jesus sat down and had a long talk about one of these subjects, what conclusions would you reach about how a person should behave? Jesus gave us direct commands such as "Forgive those who sin against you" and principles such as "Love your neighbor as yourself." It is often these principles that determine how we should or should not act or think. Can you figure out some practical ways these principles affect us in our relationships with our parents, others or ourselves?**

Conclusion and Decision

CONCLUSION (3-5 minutes)

Direct attention to the section of The Parchment headed "I Obey God . . . ". Tell students, **Read the statements and circle the one that is closest to your own situation. Then decide on an area in which you want to be more obedient, and fill in the information at the bottom of the page. This is for you alone to see; it's just between you and the Lord.**

Close in prayer after students have had time to work.

Distribute the Fun Page.

The Parchment

Matthew 21:28–30

Now that you've heard the story Jesus told in Matthew 21:28–30, rewrite the story as if it happened to one of the groups of people below. (If you like, you can do the story in cartoons.)

1. A father, mother and their two teenage kids.

2. An English teacher and two students.

3. A gas station owner and two young employees.

4. Your Bible study leader and two kids that are in your group right now.

I Obey God . . .

Circle the response that is most like your own.

1. Because I'm scared of the consequences if I don't.

2. Because God will reward me if I do.

3. Only when I want to.

4. Because I'm convinced God knows best, even if I don't always understand.

5. Because church friends wouldn't like me if I didn't.

6. Because my parents would be ashamed of me if I didn't.

7. Because God loves me and I love Him.

   I want to be more obedient in . . .

ACME YELLOW STRING

There's been an explosion at the "ACME YELLOW STRING" factory! With a pen or a pencil, follow the strings from each letter in the "ACME YELLOW STRING" banner below. Some of those strings dead-end off to the sides in knots, but the rest continue on down to the seven boxes at the bottom where they spell out the answer to this question:

"This must come under the Lord's control. What is it?"

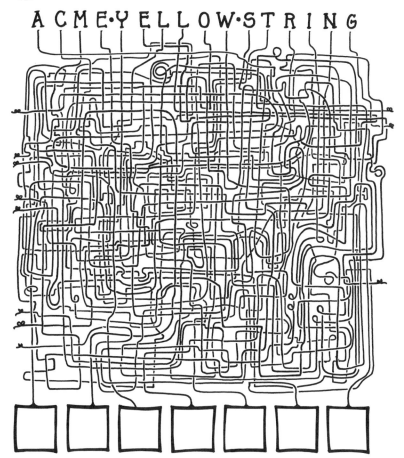

DAILY NUGGETS

Day 1 Read James 1:22-25. Why is it not enough just to hear the Word?

Day 2 Colossians 3:15-17. Think of some of the things you've done recently. How many could be done in the name of the Lord and with thanksgiving?

Day 3 John 13:12-17. What did Jesus do? How should we follow in His footsteps? List three ways you will serve others this week.

Day 4 Mark 4:21-25. What does verse 21 teach you about letting your light shine for others to see?

Day 5 Hebrews 11:8-16. What did Abraham have that helped him do what the Lord told him to do?

Day 6 Isaiah 1:18-20. Write down the result of rebelling against God. Then write the results of obedience. Which is the better choice?

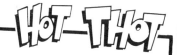

"In the same way, faith by itself, if it is not accompanied by action, is dead."

James 2:17

There's a big difference between knowing what to do, and doing it. If you want to have a living, dynamic faith in God, you have to place yourself in His hands and allow Him to take charge.

 POP SHEET

THEME: Obedience to Christ.

Session 2

BIBLE STUDY OUTLINE

Begin your message by reading Matthew 8:23-27. Ask your students what two things in verse 27 obeyed Jesus' commands (the winds and the waves). Read Mark 1:23-27. Ask what obeyed Him in verse 27 (the evil spirits). Next, read Luke 17:5,6. Point out that, although Jesus probably never actually uprooted a tree and planted it in the ocean by faith, He could have if He had wanted to. Now go to the OBJECT LESSON.

OBJECT LESSON: FREE WILL VS. OBEDIENCE

Bring a tame, friendly pet such as a kitten, puppy or turtle to show your students. As you hold the animal (or place it in sight on the floor or table), command the pet to do some simple tricks. Provide a box to place the animal in when through.

After attempting several tricks, say something to the animal like, **Well I guess you don't want to cooperate. Hey, I'm supposed to be the master! You're supposed to obey. Why won't you obey me?**

Ask your students to explain why the animal would not obey. Answers will probably include, "Not smart enough to understand you," "Wants to play," and so forth. Guide the discussion by talking about the nature of free will.

Now remind students that the winds and waves, trees and even demons obeyed the voice of Christ—but we Christians are sometimes more like the wayward pet. Say, **By nature, we are willful, disobedient people. A sign of Christian maturity is the act of obeying God even when it's hard or inconvenient. This kind of obedience is the kind that we must continually practice, for it's the only way to be the sort of people God wants us to be.** Point out some of the advantages of obedience to the Lord.

DISCUSSION QUESTIONS

1. What is free will? How do the terms "free will" and "responsible behavior" fit together? Name some things that a Christian should choose not to do. Are these things tough to turn away from?

2. Why isn't it easy or automatic for us to obey God? In other words, why doesn't the free will of most people tend to bring them close to God rather than away from God?

3. Why do you think God gave us free will?

4. Will there ever come a time when God will remove our ability to say no to Him? At least for non-Christians, the answer is yes.

 NOTES

THE COMPLETE
JUNIOR HIGH BIBLE STUDY
RESOURCE BOOK #3

Fun things to do with a VCR.

LIFESTYLES OF THE MIDDLE CLASS AND UNKNOWN

Go to the houses of several of your group members and allow them to conduct a tongue-in-cheek video-taping tour of their bedrooms, yards and so on. Interview parents and siblings. Show the videos at a special meeting, or show them one at a time over a period of a few weeks at your regular midweek meeting or game time.

PREMIER NIGHT

Schedule a special movie party. Show either a rented movie or a junior high action film you and your group made together. Also show cartoons and film, tape or slides of youth group action events. Junior high action films are easy to make and when they are shown, the "stars" tend to invite a lot of their friends. Subjects for films could be silly versions of "Robin Hood" (taped in a forest with bows and arrows and girls to rescue), Clint Eastwood cowboy movies (rent some horses at a camp), and any sort of monster movie. The secret to making a good junior high movie is to keep the plot simple. Just lots of battle scenes (red food coloring for blood) and a happy ending.

TIME CAPSULE

This one is a meaningful experience, rather than a game. At the beginning of the school year, or some other significant date, video tape the verbalized thoughts and feelings of the members of your youth group. Give each person about thirty seconds to respond to questions such as, "What are your goals for this year?" and "Why did you become a Christian?" At the end of the school year, show the interviews. The audience will probably have a few laughs—and a few tears.

Pride and Humility

INSIGHTS FOR THE LEADER

WHAT THE SESSION IS ABOUT

Pride can damage a Christian's life.

SCRIPTURE STUDIED

Job 32:1; Psalm 36:2; Proverbs 16:5; 27:2; Matthew 13:15; 15:8,9; Luke 18:9-14; Galatians 6:3.

KEY PASSAGE

"Everyone who exalts himself will be humbled, and he who humbles himself will be exalted." Luke 18:14

AIMS OF THE SESSION

During this session your learners will:

1. Study attitudes of pride and humility described in Luke 18:9-14;
2. Discuss how pride is reflected by young people today;
3. Examine their personal attitudes towards God and others.

This session focuses on a believer's attitudes towards others and God. These attitudes are sometimes revealed in prayer. The parable of Jesus that is examined in this session teaches proper attitudes not only in prayer but in our whole way of thinking about God. The length of prayer, the form of prayer and the proper words in prayer are not emphasized. God is not impressed with our many words or with proper form. He is concerned about our attitude of heart. People are concerned with the outward appearance of things, but God is concerned with the heart.

The Pharisee and the Tax Collector

To teach us about our heart attitudes, Jesus told a parable. It was directed specifically to those "who were confident of their own righteousness and looked down on everybody else" (Luke 18:9). It warned against overconfidence in one's self-righteousness which results in a "better than thou" attitude.

Jesus told of two men who went to the Temple to pray. One was a Pharisee, the other a tax collector. No one would be surprised to see the Pharisee going to the Temple for prayer, for these men prayed four times a day: at 9 A.M., 12 noon, 3P.M. and 6P.M. But Jesus' hearers would have been shocked that a tax collector would be in the Temple for prayer. Tax collectors who worked for the hated government in Rome and who gouged the public by overcharging and keeping the excess, were considered to be on a level with robbers and murderers. By speaking of a Pharisee and a tax collector, Jesus set up a contrast between a devout religious leader and a known sinner. The questions are, who is God going to hear? Who will have his prayers answered? Who will be justified (forgiven)?

Everyone hearing of these two men would naturally conclude that the "good" man, the Pharisee, would surely be heard by God. The word "Pharisee" literally means "the separated one." The Pharisees gave their entire lives to the study and practice of the Mosaic Law. They had begun with the codes of Exodus, Leviticus, Numbers, and Deuteronomy and amplified them to cover every aspect of life. For example, there were 400 laws concerning the keeping of the Sabbath. There were even laws concerning the washing of hands: four and a half ounces (135 milliliters) of water was poured over both hands and each hand was cleansed by rubbing it with the fist of the other. Then the hands were held up so that the water could drain off the wrists. The entire process was repeated, with hands being held down so that the water would drain off the fingers. This ritual was repeated between all courses of the meal. Because of this sort of meticulous observance of laws, the Pharisees

NOTES

were considered by all to be the most holy of men. They were the spiritual elite of Jesus' day.

The Pharisee in the parable stood so that others would be impressed. He prayed about himself, telling God how good he was. He began by boasting, "God, I thank you that I am not like other men" (Luke 18:11). The self-righteous are always self-centered, feeding on pride in their accomplishments. Four times the Pharisee used "I." He implied, "I need no forgiveness, no mercy, no grace. I am not a sinner like a robber or adulterer." He recognized the tax collector and said in a loathing voice, "nor even this tax collector." He boasted about his fasting and giving. Pharisees fasted twice a week, 104 times a year, although the Old Testament only prescribed one fast per year (see Lev. 16:29). He even tithed on things not required by the Law.

What the Pharisee did was good. It is beneficial to have strong spiritual discipline and to give to the Lord. It is good to keep the Ten Commandments. But his prayer was hindered because he practiced good things in order to feed his pride. He trusted in his goodness, not the goodness of God. He condemned others, comparing their works to his. He tried to make his righteousness shine by comparing it to others. He did not know that supreme law of loving God and loving others as himself.

The Proper Attitude

Jesus used a tax collector to illustrate the proper attitude. How odd that the one furthest from God would practice genuine prayer. The tax collector for the Roman government purchased the right to be a tax collector. Rome established the taxes for an area and anything the tax collector got over that sum was his. There were three taxes he would collect from everyone: a poll tax for living in an area, a land tax of one-tenth of crops or income, and an export/import tax. The tax collector could stop any man any time to collect the taxes. The tax collectors were hated and despised as both traitors and thieves.

We are told that this tax collector "would not even look up to heaven, but beat his breast" (Luke 18:13). He had an attitude of humility when he prayed. No person is worthy in himself or herself to come into the presence of God through prayer. The tax collector's confession was, "God, have mercy on me, a sinner." The original Greek text shows that the tax collector regarded himself as the chief sinner. Even the great saints regarded themselves as sinners before God. Isaiah confessed, " 'Woe to me!' I cried. 'I am ruined! For I am a man of unclean lips . . . and my eyes have seen the King, the Lord Almighty' " (Isa. 6:5). Paul wrote, "Christ Jesus came into the world to save sinners—of whom I am the worst" (1 Tim. 1:15).

Jesus said that it was not the religious man who was justified. All of his righteous acts were nullified by his wrong attitude. In contrast, the tax collector had no good works, no self-righteousness. But he was justified, forgiven as if he had never sinned. He received mercy, forgiveness and grace. True humility leads to God.

At the conclusion of the parable, Jesus gave a universal truth: "For everyone who exalts himself will be humbled, and he who humbles himself will be exalted" (Luke 18:14).

Many Christians need to learn the lesson given by Jesus. They reflect an attitude of pride in their holier-than-thou approach to other people. They tend to feel, "I'm a better person than you are because I do this and I don't do that."

These people fail to recognize the areas in which they are still weak. They are proud because of their achievements or their good works or because they don't goof off like others.

But this pride destroys many of the positive benefits of their achievements and their desirable traits. Pride can lead people to develop the attitude that they don't need God. "I'm doing so well, doing such a good job, why bother with God?"

These are the people who need to learn that in the long run, the prideful will be humbled, while those with true humility will be lifted up.

SESSION PLAN

BEFORE CLASS BEGINS: Give yourself enough time before students arrive to copy onto your chalkboard the comparison chart from the Teaching Resource page (which follows this SESSION PLAN). There is no Parchment worksheet for this session.

Attention Grabber

ATTENTION GRABBER (1 minute)

Materials needed: A scrap of wood or board (one that is termite-ridden or worm-eaten is preferred but not necessary).

When class begins, show the wood to your students. Say something like, **If you've ever seen a termite-infested piece of wood or tree, you know the damage these little creatures can do. Termites slowly chew away until the wood is weak and worthless.**

These past few sessions we've been looking at some of the parables of Jesus. We saw that the only safe foundation for a life is Jesus Christ Himself. We saw that we need to build our lives according to the blueprints that God provides. Today we're going to look at the termite of pride, which can destroy a life just as termites can destroy a building.

Bible Exploration

EXPLORATION (25-30 minutes)

Materials needed: Chalkboard or poster paper on which you have copied the comparison chart from the Teaching Resource page.

Step 1 (8-10 minutes): Read, or have a volunteer read, Luke 18:9-14. Then lead a discussion based on the comparison chart on the chalkboard. Help the students come to a detailed understanding of the events of the passage.

Step 2 (10-12 minutes): Now say, **The Pharisee was a sick man—sick with the effects of pride and arrogance, that is. Let's have some fun by pretending that we are a team of doctors and medical specialists and that the Pharisee has come to us seeking help for his illness. The first thing we must do is examine the patient so that we can diagnose his exact problem.**

As you speak, draw a picture on your chalkboard similar to this illustration:

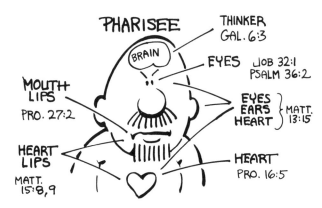

Ask a volunteer to read one of the passages on the chalkboard illustration. Jot down the important points of the passage, and lead a discussion about the meaning and significance of the passage as you write. Do this for all of the passages listed. When you discuss each passage, urge students to share some of the things young people do that relate to what the Scriptures say.

Finally, ask your learners what is their "medical opinion" of the Pharisee's spiritual condition—good or bad? The answer, of course, is very bad.

Step 3 (5-7 minutes): Now the "doctors" are to "prescribe medication." That is, allow your students to contribute their thoughts about what the Pharisee should do to become spiritually healthy. Lead the class to a basic understanding of humility by reading again about the humble tax collector in Luke 18:9-14. Refer to the INSIGHTS FOR THE LEADER section (especially under the heading "The Proper Attitude") for further insights.

Thank your students for their contributions.

Conclusion and Decision

Note: There are a few special materials required for the next session, session 4. See "BEFORE CLASS BEGINS," page 46.

Your students may wish to see this solution to the Fun Page Puzzle.

(If you like, write the solution on an extra copy of the Fun Page and pin it to your classroom bulletin board.)

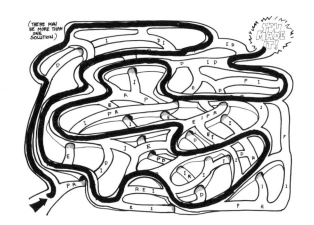

CONCLUSION: (2-4 minutes)

Comment, **We have seen how the attitude of pride, like termites in a house or a disease in a sick person, can destroy the life we are trying to build on the foundation of Christ. We all need to check our own attitudes from time to time to make sure we are not getting those termites or germs.**

Instruct your learners to describe on a blank sheet of paper, individually and privately, three or four times they have let pride get the better of them. Give them a moment of silent prayer to ask God to help them be free of pride and arrogance and to ask Him to alert them when they are giving in to prideful attitudes. Close in prayer and distribute the Fun Page.

Luke 18:9-14 Comparison Chart

	Pharisee	Tax collector
1. Why did each man pray?		
2. Name specific things each man prayed about.		
3. What opinion did each man have about himself?		
4. What did each man think that God would do?		
5. Did he go home forgiven? Why or why not?		

THE PRIDE TRIP

"Pride goes before destruction, a haughty spirit before a fall."
Proverbs 16:18

This verse from Proverbs is one of God's laws. Eventually, the proud and arrogant self-destruct. It pays, then, to remember the words of Luke 18:14, which is in the Hot Thot below. To help you remember, try our humble maze.

Instructions: Your job is to draw a line from the start to the finish that does not cross the letters P, R, I, D, and E. If you cross all of those letters (in any order) before reaching the finish, you lose. If you cross none or only some of them, you win. To keep track of which letters you've crossed, check them off on the word PRIDE in the title at the top of this page. Notice that there are several copies of each letter in the maze. You can cross as many as you like, as long as you don't ever complete the word PRIDE.

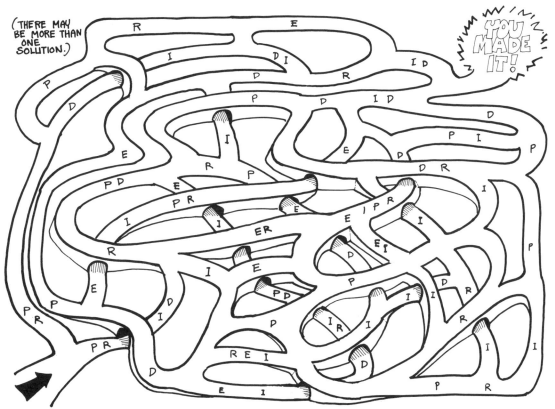

(THERE MAY BE MORE THAN ONE SOLUTION.)

YOU MADE IT!

DAILY NUGGETS

Day 1 Read 1 Peter 5:5,6. What attitude displeases God? What does He give us when we are humble?

Day 2 Luke 14:11; 18:9-14. Why is humility something we would want to develop in our lives?

Day 3 James 4:6-10. Write verses 7-10 in your own words in a way that applies to your life.

Day 4 Proverbs 16:18. Can you think of a time when pride has gotten you into trouble? What might have happened if you had been humble?

Day 5 Revelation 3:17-19. Why do you think it is harder for a rich person to be humble?

Day 6 1 John 2:15-17. What does John warn against? When we humbly obey God, what is our reward?

"Everyone who exalts himself will be humbled, and he who humbles himself will be exalted."
Luke 18:14

THEME: Pride and humility.

BIBLE STUDY OUTLINE

Read 2 Timothy 3:1-5 to your students. Make the following points as time allows:

- VERSE 1: "The last days" refers to the time shortly before Christ's return to earth. Paul tells us that the last days will be "terrible times."
- VERSES 2-4: This list of horrible things can be summed up in a word: self-centered. People have always tended to be self-centered. But apparently it's going to become worse and worse as the day of Christ's return approaches. And as it gets worse, it will be harder for the Christian to remain God-centered. As human beings, we often follow the crowd. That is, we do the things our friends do; we want to be like our friends. And if all our friends are self-centered, seeking only their own pleasures and gratification, we find it hard to stand alone for God. That's one important reason why we should surround ourselves with people who love Jesus. We need the help and support of Christian friends.
- VERSE 5: Paul tells us to avoid these proud, arrogant people. He tells us to have "nothing to do with them." In other words, we are not to be self-centered. God wants us to be God-centered.

Read 1 Peter 5:4-6. Point out the following:

- VERSE 4: Notice that Peter is talking about the last days, just as Paul was. Peter speaks of a reward for Christian behavior that Jesus will bring when He comes again.
- VERSE 5: So in the context of the final days, Peter tells us to clothe ourselves with humility. Both Peter and Paul discuss pride and humility in the light of the end times. Why? Because the most important thing to God is that the people He created center themselves on Him. A self-centered person is a person who has turned away from God. God wants to be God. He wants to be your God. But if you are self-centered, how can He be your God? When Jesus suddenly returns in great power and glory to this planet, He will force self-centered people to become God-centered. No one will be able to ignore Christ or God. Those who must be forced to focus on God will be punished. Those who choose now to be God-centered will be rewarded and honored.
- VERSE 6: Verse 6 speaks of this reward. It says that Christ will lift us up in due time. That means that if we humble ourselves to God now, eventually He will reward us with honor. I don't know about you, but that's a day I look forward to.

STORY: ALEXANDER THE GREAT

Alexander the Great was a Greek who conquered most of the civilized world back before the time of Christ. A story is told about the time he and his army came to conquer a certain city. The city was protected by a great wall. It would have taken months or even years to surround the wall and starve the people out. And the wall was too powerfully built to allow an army to penetrate.

But Alexander had a plan. He walked up to the front gate with a few dozen men. He shouted to the people staring down at him from the top of the wall. "I want to see your king," he ordered. Eventually the king appeared. "Surrender," Alexander demanded. The king and the townspeople laughed. Who did this upstart think he was? Did he believe the great city would give in to a few dusty soldiers?

"Why should we surrender to you?" the king shouted. With that, Alexander ordered his soldiers to line up single file. He then marched them toward the edge of a cliff. As the townspeople watched in horror, the soldiers marched one by one off the cliff to their deaths on the rocks below. After several men had fallen, Alexander ordered the remainder of his company to halt and return to his side.

The king surrendered the town to Alexander without a battle. You see, the king knew that if Alexander could command such fanatical loyalty among these few men, he could command it among a great army—men who would level the city and kill its residents without hesitation.

The soldiers were fools, in my opinion. But they were loyal, that's for sure. They were Alexander-centered, you might say. They gave up their own lives to follow him.

I don't want you to be fanatics. But I do want you to be loyal to God. Imagine the impact this group could have on our town if we all were as devoted to our Lord as the soldiers were to Alexander. Be God-centered.

DISCUSSION QUESTIONS:

1. **Do the people mentioned in 2 Timothy 3:1-5 sound like people today?**

2. **Why is it sometimes easier to follow the crowd than to follow Jesus? What can the members of this group do to support each other?**

3. **What would you say to a Christian friend who seems to be growing arrogant?**

4. **What sort of reward do you think God will give us for focusing our lives on Him?**

GAMES & THINGS

Messy fun with pump-style toothpaste tubes.

Important: Some toothpaste pumps are hard to start because they have air bubbles. Test all pumps before handing them to players. If a pump doesn't work, bang it against a table.

PUMP TOOTHPASTE RACE

Assemble kids into two or three teams. Give each team one toothpaste pump. On the signal to begin, contestants race to see which team can first empty their tube. These pumps quickly tire a person's thumb; allow team members to pass the tube around so that everyone has a chance to pump and a chance to rest. The various brands of toothpastes in these pumps tend to be particularly messy and sticky, so provide bowls to pump the paste into, and wet washcloths for cleanup.

SIGN IN PLEASE

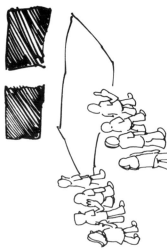

This is a relay race that is a good way for kids to get to know everybody's name. Tape big sheets of black (or other dark color) paper to the wall, and place a drop cloth on the floor below the paper. Assemble participants into two or more teams. Line the teams up as shown, and give the first player on each team a toothpaste pump that contains white toothpaste. At the signal to start, players with the pumps run to the black paper and print their first names with the toothpaste. When finished, players run back to their teams and give the pump to the next players in line. The first team to list all of its players' names is the winner.

Before teams are assembled, it's a good idea to line all players up according to the number of letters in their first names. Then, as teams are formed, you can achieve a balance so that no team is at a disadvantage.

SNAIL TRAILS

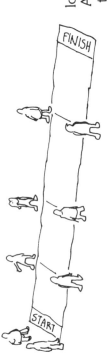

Lay a sheet of butcher paper about 20 feet long as illustrated. Each team chooses one representative who, at the signal, races the distance, creating a continuous trail of toothpaste as he or she goes. The first one to cross the "Finish" wins, but the trail of toothpaste must be unbroken or that player is disqualified.

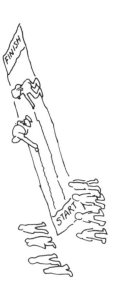

You can also involve all players by making the track longer and placing contestants along its length as shown. As one player reaches the end of his or her section of the track, he or she passes the pump to the next player.

The Light From Your House

INSIGHTS FOR THE LEADER

WHAT THE SESSION IS ABOUT

Christians' lives should reflect God's working in us.

SCRIPTURE STUDIED

Matthew 5:14-16.

KEY PASSAGE

"In the same way, let your light shine before men, that they may see your good deeds and praise your Father in heaven." Matthew 5:16

AIMS OF THE SESSION

During this session your learners will:

1. Define the meaning of "light of the world";
2. Explain how to be a "light" to other people;
3. List situations in which they can be better reflections of Christ.

The topic for this session is Jesus' statement to His disciples, "You are the light of the world" (Matt. 5:14). This is an example of "parabolic sayings" used by Jesus to make a point. A parabolic saying makes use of everyday facts well-known by the audience.

When Jesus told His disciples that they were the light of the world, He did so knowing that God is light (see 1 John 1:5; Jas. 1:17) and that He Himself, the Son, was sent forth to be "the light of the world" (see Matt. 4:16; John 1:4,9; 8:12; 9:4,5; 12:35,36).

Light comes from its own source, or from a reflection of a source. The reason we as Christ's followers can be like lights to the world is that God has given us the capacity to receive light from Him through Christ. We reflect and project God's light much as the moon or the planets shine by the light of the sun. Because Christ is in us, we receive God's transmission of light, and we are to beam that light as would a bright lamp on a tall lampstand.

Make sure students understand that the Christian's light is a derived light. It is God's light with which others must be dazzled. The glory must go to Him. The lamp is not to be the center of focus. You don't turn on a lamp in your room in order to look at and admire the lamp; you turn it on so that you can see by its light. Similarly, Christians are to provide the light that will help others "see" the way to God. Light causes darkness to vanish. In much

the same way the very presence and nature of God simply repels sin. Obviously the more light we have, the less darkness. Likewise, the more we take on God's nature the less room sin has to grow in us.

The function of light is to enable us to see where we are going and to know clearly what we are doing in the spiritual realm. This process also reveals some unpleasant truths about ourselves and our surroundings. It is clear that by showering us with His light He is not attempting to limit us, but to help us see what is really there, hidden in the cloak of darkness.

Jesus said, "Neither do people light a lamp and put it under a bowl. Instead they put it on its stand, and it gives light to everyone in the house" (Matt. 5:15). The reason for turning on a lamp is to let the light shine. God puts Christians into the world to be lights. We are to reflect His light to others so that they will praise Him.

There are sometimes barriers thrown around our light that keep it from doing the job it was meant to do. Poor choice of friends, lack of self-control, poor devotional habits, bad attitudes, selfishness and many other diversions can throw a dark shade on our light to the world.

As we free ourselves from the barriers blocking our light we can find many opportunities to reflect Christ in an accurate way. Young people can shine for Jesus at home, at school,

in their free-time activities, in church programs—in fact, wherever they go. A "shining light" Christian at home will be cooperative, obedient to parents, kind to brothers and sisters. At school the Christian will be courteous to others and will exclude no one from his or her friendship. This "shining light" will try to do his or her best in studies and will cooperate with teachers and coaches. The same attitudes of love, kindness and caring for the rights and needs of others will be manifested in clubs, sports and just "hanging around" with friends. Christians who let their lights shine will attract others to the light who is Jesus.

SESSION PLAN

BEFORE CLASS BEGINS: Photocopy enough Parchment worksheets for each student to have one. Follow the instructions on the Teaching Resource page which immediately follows the Parchment. See the CREATIVE ALTERNATIVE to the ATTENTION GRABBER for special materials required.

Attention Grabber

ATTENTION GRABBER (2-3 minutes)

Materials needed: The Teaching Resource page, cut apart as described on the page.

As students enter the classroom, give each student one of the slips you've cut from the Teaching Resource page. Tell students that they are to solve the riddle on the slips, and that there are a total of three different kinds of slips. Instruct your learners to mill around until they've each had a chance to read all three slips. The first student to give the correct answer is the winner. The answer is "light."

Make a transition to the EXPLORATION by commenting on the importance of light for daily activities; explain that this session will explore something Jesus said about His followers being light.

CREATIVE ALTERNATIVE (5-10 minutes)

Materials needed: Scarves or bandannas to serve as blindfolds; candy bar or other edible reward.

Explain, **We're going to have a race to see who can be the first to get across the room blindfolded and find the candy bar I'll place on the other side.** Show the candy bar to students and continue, **The first one to find it can keep it. Some of you will be blindfolded and will have to move across the room without being able to see. The rest of you will stand on the sidelines. The spectators can call directions to the blindfolded people.** (You may want to warn the superintendent about this one.) **But you who are blindfolded won't know whether the other people are giving you good instructions or are trying to confuse you. You won't really know whom to believe.**

Select students to be blindfolded by choosing those whose birthday is nearest to today. Make sure the blindfold is 100 percent effective. After the students are blindfolded, place the candy bar opposite them in plain sight. If you like, spin the players to make them slightly dizzy. Move the other students to the sides of the room and let the "race" begin. End the activity when one student has found the candy bar. If five minutes have elapsed and no one has found it, end the activity without a winner, and give the reward to the closest person.

Make a transition to the next part of the session by commenting on the obvious difference between darkness and light, and how light helps us avoid confusion and shows us the right path. Explain that this session will focus on something Jesus said about His followers being light.

Bible Exploration

EXPLORATION: (20-25 minutes)

Step 1 (5-7 minutes): One person in the class should read Matthew 5:14-16 aloud while the rest follow in their own Bibles. Ask the following questions, jotting students' responses on your chalkboard.

1. **What do you think Jesus meant by saying, "You are the light of the world"?**
2. **Who is the true light?**
3. **How do you think we become lights ourselves?**

Commend and underscore thoughtful and appropriate answers. Correct any inaccurate ideas, using material from INSIGHTS FOR THE LEADER.

Step 2 (6-8 minutes): Erase your chalkboard if necessary, and write on it these three headings: Sources of Light; Things that Block Light; Things that Prevent Christians from Shining.

Explain, **In the left column let's list all the possible sources of light that we can think of. Then in the middle column I want you to tell me all the things you can think of that could block that light. In the last column I want you to tell me what prevents a Christian from shedding the light that he or she has.**

Allow students to share their thoughts. Ask, **What are some ways that we can prevent our "light" from being blocked?** Let volunteers respond.

Step 3 (7-10 minutes): Tell students to look at their Parchment worksheets. Read Situation 1 to your class, and lead a discussion based on the situation and the questions that follow it on the worksheet. Do this for all three situations, or for as many as time allows.

NOTES

Your students may wish to see this solution to the Fun Page Puzzle.

(If you like, write the solution on an extra copy of the Fun Page and pin it to your classroom bulletin board.)

Note: See "BEFORE CLASS BEGINS" on page 59.

Conclusion and Decision

CONCLUSION (2-3 minutes)

Direct attention to the section of the Parchment titled, "I Need to Shine For." Instruct students, **Think about people who need to see Christ in your life. They may be family members, people at school, people on your team or in your club. Write the names of three of them. Then pray silently that our Lord will help you do a better job of reflecting His light to these people.**

Close in a brief audible prayer.

Distribute the Fun Page.

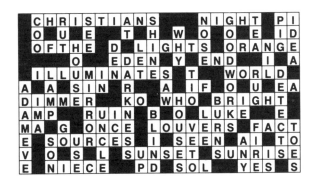

The Parchment

Let Your Light Shine

Situation 1:

About half the kids in your youth group are really trying to be the Christians Jesus wants them to be. But the rest of the kids are just "fakin' it." They are there for the fun events and games. They don't care about Jesus at all.

1. How do the things Jesus said about the light relate to this situation?

2. What could you do to help one or two of these "fakin' it" kids?

Situation 2:

Your big sister has been blowing it: she's been sneaking out the window at night to go see her boyfriend. You're not only concerned about her deception, but about what she may be doing with her boyfriend.

1. How do you think Jesus would deal with your sister if He could talk to her face to face?

2. What do you think He would want you to do for your sister?

3. What could you do if your sister did not respond to you?

Situation 3:

During lunch in the school cafeteria, a kid trips and splashes a chocolate shake all over your friend sitting next to you. Your friend goes bananas, screaming and swearing at the kid who tripped.

1. Name something you could do or say immediately that would "shine some light" into the situation.

2. What could you do later in a quiet moment that would help your friend?

I Need to Shine for:

Write the names of three people who need to see Jesus in your life. Then write some simple things you could do to let His light shine in their lives.

Teaching Resource 4 **Instructions: Cut apart all the slips on this page (if you expect more than twelve students in your class, make enough photocopies of this page for each student to have one slip.)**

Solve this riddle: "Part of the time I come for free, the rest of the time you pay for me. What am I?"	**Solve this riddle:** "I am faster than the fastest thing, but if I run into you, you'll feel no sting. What am I?"	**Solve this riddle:** "Here's a tough one— I come in waves, but I'm not the ocean. What am I?"
Solve this riddle: "Part of the time I come for free, the rest of the time you pay for me. What am I?"	**Solve this riddle:** "I am faster than the fastest thing, but if I run into you, you'll feel no sting. What am I?"	**Solve this riddle:** "Here's a tough one— I come in waves, but I'm not the ocean. What am I?"
Solve this riddle: "Part of the time I come for free, the rest of the time you pay for me. What am I?"	**Solve this riddle:** "I am faster than the fastest thing, but if I run into you, you'll feel no sting. What am I?"	**Solve this riddle:** "Here's a tough one— I come in waves, but I'm not the ocean. What am I?"
Solve this riddle: "Part of the time I come for free, the rest of the time you pay for me. What am I?"	**Solve this riddle:** "I am faster than the fastest thing, but if I run into you, you'll feel no sting. What am I?"	**Solve this riddle:** "Here's a tough one— I come in waves, but I'm not the ocean. What am I?"

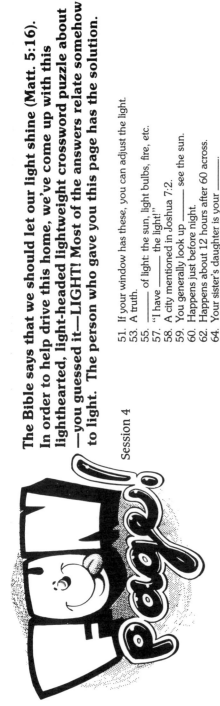

The Bible says that we should let our light shine (Matt. 5:16). In order to help drive this home, we've come up with this lighthearted, light-headed lightweight crossword puzzle about —you guessed it—LIGHT! Most of the answers relate somehow to light. The person who gave you this page has the solution.

Session 4

ACROSS

1. When Jesus says, "You are the light of the world" (Matt. 5:14), who does He mean?
6. Comes after day.
9. 3.14159.
12. Short for "identity."
13. "You are the light _____ world." (Matt. 5:14. Two words.)
16. "Turn on the _____."
17. A color in the rainbow.
19. The garden of _____ (Gen. 2:8).
21. Finish
22. A shining light _____ the subject.
28. We are to be the light of the _____ (Matt. 5:14).
32. What a sinner commits.
33. "What _____?"
34. Short for "each."
35. A device for turning the lights down.
37. In boxing, when a fighter "punches your lights out," it's a _____.
38. _____, what, where, when, why.
40. The opposite of "dim."
42. In electrical terms; a unit of current (abbreviated form).
43. To destroy, or an ancient damaged site.
47. The Gospel of _____
48. Not your pa, but your _____
50. One less than twice.

51. If your window has these, you can adjust the light.
53. A truth.
55. _____ of light: the sun, light bulbs, fire, etc.
57. "I have _____ the light!"
58. A city mentioned in Joshua 7:2.
59. You generally look up _____ see the sun.
60. Happens just before night.
62. Happens about 12 hours after 60 across.
64. Your sister's daughter is your _____
65. Short for "Police Dept."
66. An old-fashioned name for the sun.
67. Opposite of "no."

DOWN

1. A sound doves make.
2. If your life is routine and boring, you're in a _____ .
3. Your eyes need light to _____.
4. The sun doesn't shine _____ night.
5. What the sun does during the day.
6. When someone understands something, you might say, "That's it! You've hit on the _____!"
7. In many versions of the Bible, Matt. 5:16 says we are to let our light shine so people will see our _____ (two words).
8. A drink similar to coffee.
9. An animal mentioned in the Bible.
10. If a light bulb appears over your head, it means you have a bright _____ .
11. Who, what, where, when, _____.
14. In a storm, sailors look for a light _____.
15. When Daniel was put in it, it was probably dark in the lions' _____. (Dan. 6:16)
16. An old song: "This little light of mine, I'm gonna _____ it shine."
18. A word meaning "nothing" or "of no effect."
20. "Light has come into the world, but men loved _____ instead of light" (John 3:19, NASB).
23. "Your word is a _____ to my feet" (Psalm 119:105).
24. You look at your reflection in this.
25. "But if we walk _____ the light . . . " (1 John 1:7).
26. Past tense of "see."
27. Spanish for 44 down.
29. If you want to hide something in the darkness, you could sweep it _____ under the _____.
30. This is what a detective does.
31. These two were the original people in the garden of Eden: _____ and _____
36. Short for "I am a."
39. Plural of 14 down.
40. If you come too close to fire, you may suffer _____
41. Short for "in other words," in Latin that is.
44. Your father's brother is your _____.
45. Frozen water.
46. Persons who cannot see are _____
47. A boy's name.
49. The opposite of "stop."
52. The president says no to a bill.
53. This will burn you.
54. You probably have five of these on your foot.
55. Jesus is the _____ of God.
56. To "employ," something. For example, a hammer.
58. "_____ and all."
61. Opposite of down.
63. "Who _____ it?"

DAILY NUGGETS

Day 1 Read Luke 11:33–36. What part of the body is the lamp? What happens when it is good?

Day 2 Ephesians 5:8–14. How should we walk as children of the light?

Day 3 Philippians 2:14,15. How should we do things? What should we become?

Day 4 1 Timothy 4:12. In what ways are young Christians to be examples? How could you be a good example this week?

Day 5 1 Peter 2:9. What does Peter say Christians are? What are they to do? Are you doing this?

Day 6 Matthew 5:14. How will you be a light to someone this week?

HOT TO HOT

"In the same way, let your light shine before men, that they may see your good deeds and praise your Father in heaven." Matthew 5:16

 **POP SHEET**

THEME: Christians' lives should reflect God's light.

Session 4

BIBLE STUDY OUTLINE

Read John 8:12 to your listeners. Stress the fact that Christians have Jesus in their lives, and therefore have His light. Describe the nature of light (it illuminates, reveals, exposes, brings to attention) and compare it to the spiritual light that Christians have.
Now read Philippians 2:14,15. Make the following points:

- We are to be blameless and pure, two things that are seemingly rare in our time. And we are to be without fault in a crooked and perverse generation. In other words, we are to stand out like sore thumbs! Or as the Bible puts it, we are to shine "like stars in the universe." It is never easy to take a stand against the majority of people. It's not easy to say to a good friend, "No, I won't do that because I'm a Christian," or "I want to be like this and do this good thing because I am a Christian." But that's what Christ calls us to do. We are to be different. We are to shine like lights. Christ's light is to shine through us. (*Now go to the OBJECT LESSON.*)

 **NOTES**

OBJECT LESSON: SIN SACKS

Materials needed: A table lamp with the shade removed to expose the bare light bulb; extension cord if needed; several paper lunch sacks; a felt marker. Note: This object lesson works best in a darkened room.

Plug in and turn on the lamp for all to see. Again talk about the nature of the light it casts; how it illuminates, helps us see, and so on. Now hold up one of the sacks. Say, **This sack represents sin**. Label a common sin on the sack with the marker, such as "Bad Language." **When I place this sin sack over the light, see what happens. It dims the light and makes it much harder to see.** Leave the sack on the light bulb. Take another sack and again label it with another common sin (ask the crowd to make suggestions). Cover the first sack with the second. Do this several times until the light is completely blocked. Discuss the nature of sin and the way it can block a Christian's effectiveness and purpose. Talk about confession and forgiveness of sin, removing the sacks one by one as you do.

Wrap up the message by describing how a person who shines with God's light can make a positive and important impact in the lives of other people.

DISCUSSION QUESTIONS

1. **What do the words *blameless* and *pure* mean? How can we be that way?**

2. **In what ways is our generation crooked and perverse?**

3. **Name several practical ways a Christian can shine God's light on friends or family.**

4. **How can we help each other when we find it hard to shine or stay blameless and pure?**

Silly stuff.

BATTLE OF THE BANDS

Participants form musical bands and play "instruments" such as pots and pans from the church kitchen, bottles partially filled with water, whistles made of grass held in the hands, and anything else they can think of. You might give a few kazoos to each group. Each band follows an adult leader into a separate room or area where they choose a popular song and practice their performance. Each band has a chance to play before the entire group. Judges award silly prizes to the winners of various categories. Categories can include "Most Obnoxious Sound," "Hardest to Recognize Song," and so forth.

TRASH MAN

Slave parties based on attendance contests aren't as popular as they used to be, but they are a lot of fun. One of the games often played at the typical slave party was a "bidding war" for slaves whose identities were hidden. If you want to play this game, take all the slaves into another room. One at a time, bring each slave out in a large trash can, covered with a lid. The crowd bids on the unknown slave (using phony money won during the previous weeks for bringing friends to church, memorizing Scripture, and so on). To motivate the bidding, you can throw some silly hints to the crowd, such as, "One of our most coordinated slaves."

STRING ALONG

Let's say you're playing a game that requires six volunteers, three who will throw the pies and three who will be hit with messy pies and three who will throw the pies. Here's a fun way to choose who gets to do what. Write each assignment on a card or piece of paper, so that you have six cards (in our hypothetical game; three that say, "You throw the pie," and three that say, "You get hit by the pie"). Now tie a roll of string to each card. Hide each card in separate rooms, as far away from the game room as the strings allow. Twist the strings around furniture and other obstacles. The loose ends of the strings are gathered together at the front of the game room. Volunteers each pick a string and follow it, with an adult supervisor if necessary, to the card on the other end.

This stunt works well with any kind of message. Try it with Bible verses during a Bible study. Or label each card with just one letter; the kids find all the letters and arrange them into the proper message.

The Open Heart

WHAT THE SESSION IS ABOUT

No reason is good enough for not responding to God's loving invitation.

SCRIPTURE STUDIED

Luke 14:15-24.

KEY PASSAGE

"For the message of the cross is foolishness to those who are perishing, but to us who are being saved it is the power of God."
1 Corinthians 1:18

AIMS OF THE SESSION

During this session your learners will:

1. Explain how the people in the parable of the banquet responded to the invitations and what the results were;

2. List excuses people use today in refusing God's invitation;

3. Pray for someone who has not responded positively or who may not yet have been invited.

INSIGHTS FOR THE LEADER

The parable found in this session is centered around a great banquet. In this parable we see both the heart of God and the heart of man revealed. God's heart is open, with His love expressed to all. Unregenerate man's heart is closed, rejecting the love of God with hollow excuses. Yet God is persistent in seeking a people for Himself.

The occasion of this parable is a dinner in the home of a Pharisee on a Sabbath day. Jesus was answering questions raised by various noted guests. He had told them a parable about seeking a seat of honor (see Luke 14:7-11). He had spoken about humility and a call to be concerned about the poor (see Luke 14:12-14).

Then a guest exclaimed, "Blessed is the man who will eat at the feast in the kingdom of God" (Luke 14:15). We do not know why he said this. We do not know if it was because he counted himself worthy to participate in the feast, or because he was moved by Jesus' acceptance of the poor and needy. Whatever the motive for the statement, we do know that many Jews of Jesus' day looked forward to enjoying the festive celebrations of heaven. The kingdom of God, described by Jesus as a banquet, is not a place of joylessness and bleakness, but one of joy and celebration. Our experience with Christ is not depressing, but enjoyable.

The Parable of the Great Banquet

Jesus responded to the guest's comment with another parable, this time emphasizing several important truths about the kingdom of God. The host in the parable sent invitations to his friends, those who knew him. According to the custom of the day, invitations were sent out and accepted well in advance of the actual day of the event. Then the host would send a servant to let the guests know when the meal was actually ready. It is this second invitation that the invited guests evidently rejected. This refusal was a serious insult to the host.

The invited guests who turned down the summons to the banquet represent those who have knowledge of God, but who refuse to come to Him on His terms. The Pharisees to whom Jesus was speaking had the greatest opportunity to know God. They studied the Law and the Prophets. They were called by God, they looked for the Messiah, and they professed a love for God and a desire to work with God. Yet when the Messiah Himself came, they then rejected His call, each with a different excuse.

"I have just bought a field, and I must go and see it," said the first friend (v. 18). This was a poor excuse. One does not buy a field without looking at it first. But, even if he hadn't seen it, he could have seen it after the banquet or waited until the next day. Furthermore, if

the banquet was held at night, it would have been difficult for this man to have seen the new field in the dark. His refusal of the invitation was really saying, "I am too busy. I don't have time." Many young people feel that they are too busy for God. School, sports, friends, jobs and family responsibilities take first place. They don't think God's banquet is worth making the extra effort.

Excuse number two was, "I have just bought five yoke of oxen, and I'm on my way to try them out" (v. 19). This, too, was a poor excuse. A sensible person would have tested the oxen before buying them. In addition, the average farmer had only two oxen, yet this man had ten (five pair). Surely he had a hired man who could have tested the oxen. Or the man could have waited until after the banquet, or until the next day. What he was really saying was that the oxen were more important to him than his friend.

Your students, too, may find possessions more important than God. New stereos, motorcycles, clothes, surfboards, skis or other objects may interfere with their relationship with God. These students don't realize how much more valuable knowing God is than having material possessions. Jesus said, "For where your treasure is, there your heart will be also" (Luke 12:34).

The third excuse made in the parable for this session was, "I just got married, so I can't come" (Luke 14:20). The friend was saying that he hadn't had time for his honeymoon yet, and staying with his wife was more important than attending the banquet. The initial invitation to the banquet must have been issued before the wedding, but after the wedding date was set, since weddings in those days were planned well ahead of time. So the man knew, when he accepted the initial invitation, that he would be newly married when the banquet came around. He accepted then, only to decline at the last minute.

This man was letting one good thing—his marriage—interfere with another—his friendship with the host. Yet there need not have been any conflict. The man surely could have honored his commitment to attend the banquet without disrupting his marriage. He simply didn't value his host highly enough to attend.

Young people today also have this sort of problem in their relationship with God. They fear that knowing Him may interfere with a relationship with a girlfriend or boyfriend. They may be concerned with what their friends will think if they follow Christ. So they decide to become a Christian later.

Same Ol' Excuses

Thus the invited guests used three excuses still in use by many today: I can't come because I am too busy. I can't come because I have a new possession. I can't come because I have a more important relationship. God calls, but I can't obey right now.

The host was justly outraged at his friends who had treated him so rudely. So he ordered the poor, the blind, the lame to be brought to the banquet. These were the rejected, the outcasts, the deformed, the people considered worthless members of society. None had any hopes of being entertained at such a feast. The respectable people of society would have nothing to do with the likes of these. Yet the host invited them to his banquet.

We see here a warning by Jesus that the rejection of the Messiah by the Jews would result in their being supplanted by the Gentiles (see Luke 20:9-19). The original guests wouldn't come, so the invitation went out to those who would accept. Those who accepted the invitation undoubtedly enjoyed a wonderful feast.

Jesus invites all to His banquet table, for He loves us all and wants us to enjoy fellowship with Him. Some respond with excuses, but others gladly receive His invitation and enjoy eternal life with Him.

SESSION PLAN

BEFORE CLASS BEGINS: Prepare index cards as explained in the ATTENTION GRABBER. Carefully read the information on the "Excuse-O-Matic" Teaching Resource page (which immediately follows the Parchment worksheet). Play the Resource page game at home, making sure you understand the rules of play. Make enough photocopies of the Resource page so that each group of two or three students has one, and enough copies of the Parchment for each student to have one.

Attention Grabber

ATTENTION GRABBER (5-7 minutes)

Materials needed: Before class, prepare index cards for students. Half the cards should say, "I'd like to _____." The other half should say, "But I can't because _____."

When you are ready to begin the activity, distribute the cards (one of each kind to each student) and say, **Do not let anyone else see what is on your cards. We're going to play a game similar to "Mad-Libs." Fill in the blank on your cards with any response you wish. Be as funny or as serious as you wish, but not rude.** Let students work for a minute, then regain their attention.

Collect the cards and put the "I'd like to _____" cards in one pile and the "But I can't because _____" cards in another. Pick one card from each pile and read as a complete statement to the class. This should result in a good bit of fun and humor.

Make a transition to the next part of the session by saying something like this: **We've heard some creative excuses just now. The parable we're going to look at today is a story about people who had some pretty lame excuses for turning down an invitation to an important banquet.**

Bible Exploration

EXPLORATION (30-40 minutes)

Step 1 (2-3 minutes): Take two or three minutes to give a brief introduction to the parable in Luke 14:15-24, using information from INSIGHTS FOR THE LEADER (especially the first few paragraphs).

NOTES

Note: The next session, session 6, requires a tape recorder and tape. See the EXPLORATION for details, page 71.

Concentrate on the background and setting of the parable; do not give to students the details of the story which they should discover for themselves.

Step 2 (8-12 minutes): Have students form groups of two or three. Direct attention to the Parchment section titled "The Servant's Report" and instruct students, **One member of your group should read aloud Luke 14:16-24 while the others follow in their own Bibles. Then follow the instructions in the Parchment worksheet to write a servant's report. Imagine that you are one of the servants who was asked to bring people to the banquet. At the end of your day's work you are filling out a report to tell what happened and how you feel about it.**

Step 3 (3-4 minutes): Reassemble the class and have a representative from each group read the group's report. Fill in any missing information about the details of the story.

Then comment briefly on the meaning of the parable—that people are invited to enjoy knowing God, but some do not respond except with various excuses.

Step 4 (5-7 minutes): Lead a discussion, asking students to suggest excuses that people give today for refusing to accept Jesus as Saviour. (You can make this step a little more fun by doing this: Draw a big target on the chalkboard labeled "Easy Excuse Finder." Tell students they are to suggest excuses to be written in sections of the target. Then, anyone who needs an excuse for not following the Lord can just throw a dart at the target!) Ideas include the following: God wrecks my fun; He has too many rules; church is boring; I'm too busy; I already have a religion; the Bible can't be trusted; I might lose my friends; I'd have to quit certain habits or activities. (Basically, all excuses tend to boil down to one thing: God will interfere with my life.)

Step 5 (10-12 minutes): Reassemble the groups, and distribute copies of the Teaching Resource game, "ACME Excuse-O-Matic," one game per group. Give each group scissors to cut out the five cards. Tell students that this is a fun and curious game they will enjoy. Go over the instructions as students read along. Mill around the room as students play, to be sure they all understand the rules. Collect the scissors.

When everyone has had several minutes to play, ask students to comment on the "I can't follow Jesus because . . . " card. Unlike the other cards, it only has one response (number 111) which says, "There is no good excuse for not following Jesus!"

Discuss the danger of using excuses to put God off. Young people sometimes say, "When I get older I'll accept Christ." But there is no guarantee they will live that long. Furthermore, a person's heart can become so hard that the Holy Spirit won't get through. People can also get themselves in a lot of trouble while living without God. Why try to sneak in to the banquet when they're clearing the tables? Much better to come in at the beginning and enjoy the full meal!

Conclusion and Decision

CONCLUSION (2-3 minutes)

Direct attention to the "Invitation List" in the Parchment. Instruct students, **Think of some people who need to be invited to know Christ. List them on the Parchment. Then decide if you are willing for God to use you to issue the invitation. If you are, write a note to that effect at the bottom of the page. Don't forget to pray for these people even if you don't have an opportunity to talk to them.**

Close in prayer. Distribute the Fun Page.

The Parchment

The Servant's Report

Read Luke 14:16-24. You are the servant asked to bring people to the feast. At the end of your day's work, fill out this report. Make sure to tell what happened and your feelings about it.

ACTIVITY LEDGER

Day ending _____ Time _____

Comments or observations

Guest #1

Guest #2

Guest #3

Invitation List

Perhaps you know some friends or relatives who need to be invited to know Christ. List them below.

PEOPLE TO INVITE TO
THE HEAVENLY BANQUET

1.

2.

3.

4.

5.

THE ACME EXCUSE-O-MATIC!

Fell asleep during class? Didn't show up on time? Sooner or later EVERYBODY blows it. But ACME has the solution! Our automatic excuse machine will supply a guaranteed high quality excuse exactly when you need it! No more stuttering and staring at the floor when your teacher asks you why you didn't do the assignment. Simply follow these instructions:

1. Cut out the five cards.   2. Read the sentence printed on each card. Pick the one card with the sentence you like and lay it off to the side.   3. Shuffle the remaining four cards and then divide them into **two pairs,** face up, like this:

Pair A   Pair B

4. Now look at PAIR A. Do the colors (black or white) of the eyes match?   5. Look at PAIR B. Do the eyes match?   6. Add up the numbers of PAIRS with **matching eyes.** If only PAIR A is a matching pair, then you have just one matching pair. If only PAIR B is a matching pair, you have just one matching pair. If both A and B match (they do not have to match each other!) then you have two matching pairs. Of course, if neither pair matches, you have no matching pairs!

7. OK, got it so far? Now write down the number of matching pairs (not cards, pairs). For example, if you have no pairs, write down a "0."

8. Now follow Steps 3 through 7 again, only this time look for matching expressions (smile or frown). When you've determined the number of pairs, write it down next to the first number.   Follow steps 3 through 7 one last time, but look for matching bow tie colors (black or white). Write down that number next to the other two. You should now have a three digit number, for example "012."   Look up that number in the **EXCUSE LIST** below. PRESTO! There's a great excuse for the card you laid to one side. That excuse applies **only** to that one card, but each card may have more than one excuse.

Try it again. It's fun. (Then try to explain how it works.)

EXCUSE LIST

000 CLASS IS BORING!
001 MY WATCH IS TEN MINUTES SLOW.
002 I WAS KNOCKED UNCONSCIOUS BY A SPIT-WAD.
010 MY MOM DIDN'T WAKE ME UP IN TIME.
012 I THOUGHT SUNDAY SCHOOL WAS ON MONDAY.
020 I STAYED UP TOO LATE WATCHING "TEENAGE WEREWOLF."
021 I HAD TO RESCUE A FAMILY FROM A BURNING BUILDING.
022 I *ALWAYS* SLEEP DURING CLASS.
100 DOING HOMEWORK IS AGAINST MY RELIGIOUS BELIEFS.
102 IT WENT THROUGH THE WASH.
111 THERE IS NO GOOD EXCUSE FOR NOT FOLLOWING JESUS!!
120 THE DOG ATE IT.
122 IT FELL OFF MY BIKE ON THE WAY HERE.
200 EVERYBODY ELSE SLEPT THROUGH CLASS.
201 WHAT LATE? EVERYBODY'S EARLY!
202 MY MOM ACCIDENTALLY GAVE ME SLEEPING PILLS INSTEAD OF VITAMINS.
210 I WENT TO THE WRONG CHURCH!
212 I THOUGHT ALL SUNDAYS ARE HOLIDAYS.
220 I WAS BITTEN BY THE DREAD "TSETSE FLY." I HAVE SLEEPING SICKNESS.
221 I HAD TO GO HOME TO GET MY BIBLE.
222 I WASN'T ASLEEP; I WAS JUST RESTING MY EYES.

THE CROSS!

The HOT THOT below tells us that Jesus' death on the cross is a very significant event for Christians. But to people who aren't saved and don't care about Jesus, it seems meaningless. Just for fun, try this simple maze. Find your way to the cross. But don't take a wrong turn, or you'll end up in "Foolish City" or some other bad place! The person who gave you this page has the solution.

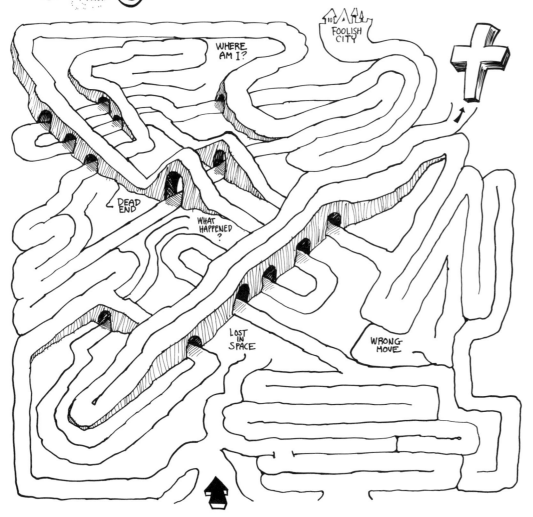

DAILY NUGGETS

Day 1 Read Matthew 11:28-30. What does verse 29 say people are to do? How does Jesus then meet our need?

Day 2 Matthew 19:16-21. Is there something too important to you to give up if Jesus asked you to? If so, ask Jesus to help you in this area.

Day 3 Mark 1:16-18. How did Simon and Andrew respond to Jesus' call? What two things did Jesus call them to do?

Day 4 Luke 9:23,24. Rewrite these verses in your own words. How can you apply this to your own life?

Day 5 Ephesians 4:11-15. From verses 13 and 15, make a list of goals that Christians should be working toward as a response to Jesus.

Day 6 Hebrews 4:15,16. Spend some time in prayer telling God how you feel about this passage.

"For the message of the cross is foolishness to those who are perishing, but to us who are being saved it is the power of God."

1 Corinthians 1:18

THEME: People who respond to God's invitation will find comfort and rest.

Session 5

BIBLE STUDY OUTLINE

Read Matthew 11:28-30 to your students. Discuss these points as time allows:

- VERSE 28: Jesus makes an invitation to everyone who is burdened and wearied by life. You have now reached the age where many of you are starting to ask important questions about life. You are asking questions such as, "What do I want from life?" or "What will I be like when I'm an adult?" As you get older, each of you will choose a direction—a philosophy of life—that you will follow. Many of you may choose to "grab all the gusto." That is, you may focus your life on money and possessions. A few of you may decide to focus on other people by helping the poor or the aged. Some of you may consider raising a family the most important aspect of your life. But whatever direction you choose, you will find that life presents you with trials and burdens. Raising a family is very hard to do—ask your folks. Seeking wealth causes worries about careers and the economy. Even helping others is hard and tiring work. In other words, life is full of burdens and problems. But Jesus invites everyone to come into His rest.

   How is Jesus able to give us rest? Mainly because He controls everything. We don't have to worry about money or anything else if He is in charge of our lives. He'll make sure everything works out.

- VERSES 29,30: But notice that Jesus says that even with Him we have a yoke and a burden. That is, Jesus does not promise to slickly and instantly solve our problems the minute we become Christians. Instead, He can help us find the solutions to the problems that we do face in life.

   What sort of burden does Jesus place on us? First John 5:3 gives us a hint. It says, "This is love for God: to obey his commands. And his commands are not burdensome." The only real burden we have is to obey God's commands. And what are His commands? To love God and to love our neighbors (see

Matt. 22:37-39). Those are happy commands, not terribly burdensome. Take Jesus' yoke and burden upon you—He will give you comfort and rest as you live your life.

OBJECT LESSON: BACKPACK OF BURDENS

When you come to the head of the class to teach, wear a backpack containing several bricks or other heavy objects. Remove the pack as you speak of burdens and allow the students to pass it around.

DISCUSSION QUESTIONS

1. **What are some of the burdens and worries you see adults facing today?**

2. **In what ways could God help solve these problems?**

3. **What are some of the burdens and worries facing kids today?**

4. **In what ways could God help solve these problems?**

5. **Why do you suppose God doesn't instantly solve all our problems when we become Christians?**

Three challengers to test your students' great talents.

VACUUM CLEANER RACES

Locate all of the electrical outlets in your game room. On the floor next to each outlet, place five bits of paper, popcorn, or any other thing that can be easily sucked up by a vacuum cleaner. Tape a sheet of paper on the wall above each outlet. Label each outlet either A or B, an equal number of both.

Ask for two volunteers, one to be assigned to all the A outlets and one for all the B outlets. Give each a vacuum cleaner. On the signal to begin, each volunteer races to his or her first assigned outlet, plugs in the cleaner and vacuums up the scraps. Contestants race from outlet to outlet, plugging in and vacuuming up the scraps. The first one done is the winner. Unless your vacuums are exactly the same, contestants will have to trade vacuums and run the course again. Sum up total elapsed time for the two runs to determine the winner. (Or use just one vacuum cleaner, racing one person at a time against the clock.)

SUCKER'S GAME

Assemble three or four teams of two players each. Sit players on the floor or at tables. Give each pair one straw and a bowl filled with an equal number (twenty or thirty) of "oyster" crackers or similar small, lightweight snack crackers. On the signal to begin, one player of each team uses the straw as a "sucking device" to pick up a cracker and drop it into his or her partner's mouth. The first team to swallow all twenty or thirty crackers wins.

It's important that the crackers are dropped into the mouths, not placed there. Otherwise, the player with the straw will suck up saliva!

SLIP AND SLIDE

As a crowd breaker, have several volunteers compete to see who can perform the most outrageous imitation of someone slipping on a banana peel. The one receiving the loudest laughs is the winner.

The Concerned Heart Session 6

INSIGHTS FOR THE LEADER

WHAT THE SESSION IS ABOUT

Christians need to be willing to have caring hearts.

SCRIPTURE STUDIED

Luke 15:1-32

KEY PASSAGE

"I tell you that in the same way there will be more rejoicing in heaven over one sinner who repents than over ninety-nine righteous persons who do not need to repent." Luke 15:7

AIMS OF THE SESSION

During this session your learners will:

1. Retell the parables of the lost sheep, lost coin, and lost son;
2. Discuss how Christians can show concern and care for those who don't know Christ personally;
3. Tell how to be found by Christ; pray for those who aren't.

In this session you and your students will be thinking about three items of great value. Each item is lost and then found. The theme of the parable is the love of God for the lost.

The Lost Sheep

The parable has three parts. The first part (Luke 15:3-7) is about a shepherd's concern for his lost sheep. Being a shepherd in Judea was a hard and dangerous job. Palestine is a rugged country full of hills and cliffs. The trails are narrow and treacherous. The pastures are scarce and small. It was easy for one of the flock to wander off or be left behind. There were no fences to restrain the sheep. And a sheep without a shepherd was defenseless against a wolf or lion. Thus a sheep left alone was doomed to death.

Only the shepherd could protect the sheep. Each lamb was the shepherd's responsibility. If a lamb was lost, it was the shepherd's job to find it, dead or alive. Then the shepherd had to bring back either the sheep or the fleece. The good shepherd would not lie down to rest until the lost was found. The shepherd spent so much time with the sheep that each one became a personal friend. When one was lost, the shepherd would leave the rest of his flock in another's care and search for the lost sheep. If he was fortunate, he would find the sheep and treat any cuts it might have with oil, then carry it home. It was the custom of the villages

to rejoice over the recovery of one lost sheep. Jesus was drawing upon this common practice in His day to tell of God's rejoicing over the finding of one lost sinner.

The Lost Coin

The next parable (Luke 15:8-10) tells of the loss of a coin. In Judea a married woman had a headdress of ten silver coins on a silver chain. Keeping this headdress was most important because it showed her faithfulness to her husband. It seems likely that this woman lost one of these coins. She was very anxious to find it. This was not an easy task in the dark Judean house. The only natural light that came into the house was from a small circular window about a foot and a half across. The floor consisted of dirt covered with dried reeds. Looking for the coin was like looking for a needle in a haystack. When the woman found her coin, she and her neighbors rejoiced. Just as there was great rejoicing over the lost sheep that was found, so there was great rejoicing over the coin which was found. And so is there rejoicing over a sinner who repents.

The Lost Son

Jesus continued the parable with the story of the lost son (see Luke 15:11-32). This third part of the parable tells of a son who wanted to leave his father. He went to his father and asked for his share of the property. He left his

home, moving to a distant country. There he spent all his money. At last he ended up working for a farmer feeding pigs. This was a job despised by Jews, for pigs were considered unclean. The son was so under-fed that he actually wanted to eat the food the pigs ate. He had hit bottom!

As he saw himself for what he really was, he came to his senses. He realized that even the servants of his father's house were treated better than he was. He determined to go home and confess his sin. Recognizing that he was not worthy to be called his father's son, he was ready to ask for a job as a servant when he went back to his father.

"But while he was still a long way off, his father saw him and was filled with compassion for him" (v. 20). The father loved his son and hoped that some-day he would return. He had not given up hope. The father "ran to his son, threw his arms around him and kissed him." Here is the love of God! For just one sin-ner returned, there is joy.

And yet, where there was joy, there was also sor-row. The elder son did not rejoice when his brother came home. In fact, he became angry (see v. 28). The father pleaded with him to come and join the cel-ebration, but he answered, "Look! All these years I've been slaving for you and never disobeyed your orders. Yet you never gave me even a young goat so I could celebrate with my friends. But when this son of yours who has squandered your property with prostitutes comes home, you kill the fattened calf for him!" (vv. 29,30).

The older brother's speech indicates that he did not share his father's loving and compassionate atti-tude. He didn't seem to love the father, either. He obeyed out of duty, and yet his mind was on roast calf and parties, not on enjoying his father's love nor his company. He shared neither his father's sorrow over the departure of the other son nor the father's joy over his return.

The sons in this parable show two kinds of sin-ners: the open sinner who runs off to do as he pleases, and the self-righteous sinner who is filled with pride, who serves without loving, who doesn't really enter into the Father's interests, but looks for what he can gain.

God does not want just servants, He wants sons. God does not want our sacrifice, He wants our love.

Unlike the sheep and the coin, which the owners could search for and reclaim, a son's heart is not sim-ply searched for. It is sought and won. God does not actually search for us. He knows where we are. His search is a desire to win our hearts with His love. That is what the cross is all about. The death and resurrec-tion of Jesus tell us of God's love. The cross captures our hearts. Our hearts would remain uncaptured if God didn't have a caring heart. "How great is the love the Father has lavished on us, that we should be called children of God!" (1 John 3:1).

Some of your students may be lost. Some, like the coin, may not know they are lost. God searches for them until He finds them. Others, like the sheep, may know they are lost but not know what to do about it. God searches for these, too, and brings them to safety.

Finally, some may be lost because they have cho-sen to be lost, like the prodigal son. Or some may be lost in their own self-centeredness, like the elder brother. The father in the parable did not track down the younger son in the distant country and drag him home. He didn't grab the elder son by the arm and march him into the house where the party was going on. He allowed each one to make his own choices and to find his own time for overcoming his lostness. We know that the prodigal came home to the father's open arms. We are not told of the elder brother's final response.

God will seek and search for those who are lost. Then He will welcome them with joy and celebration. And He will plead with those who are estranged from Him by their own self-righteousness. But He will not force anyone. His is a kingdom of love, not of com-pulsion.

SESSION PLAN

BEFORE CLASS BEGINS: You will need a cassette recorder and blank cassette for the EXPLORATION. Make enough photocopies of the Parchment for all students to have one.

Attention Grabber

ATTENTION GRABBER (5-6 minutes)

Direct attention to the Parchment worksheet. Tell students, **See if you can figure out the answer to the puzzle. After you have figured it out, answer the questions.** (The answer to the puzzle is "My contact lenses.") After allowing time for students to work, regain their attention and ask for their answers to the puzzle and to the questions. Briefly discuss the sadness people feel when they lose something important to them. Then make a transition to the EXPLORATION by saying, **The parables we are going to look at today speak about losing things and finding them again.**

Bible Exploration

EXPLORATION (25-40 minutes)

Materials needed: Sheets of newsprint; felt pens; tape recorder and blank tape.

Step 1 (10-15 minutes): Draw attention to the "Help! I'm Lost!" section of the Parchment worksheet. Read (or have one or more volunteers read) Luke 15:1-32, stopping to discuss important points and answer the questions on the worksheet. Use material from INSIGHTS FOR THE LEADER for additional background. Be sure to instruct students to write the answers on their worksheets. (Some of the Parchment's questions do not have a direct answer from Scripture. Encourage students to say what they think the answers probably are.)

Step 2 (7-10 minutes): Tell your students, **Work together in groups of three or four to prepare a script for a "teaser" or preview of a new mystery radio show called "The Case of the Missing . . . "** (Your group will finish the title based on the parable you've been working on.) **Your preview should have a cliff-hanger ending inviting listeners to tune into the Scripture to find the end of the story. At the same time see if you can work the meaning of the parable into the script. Don't forget to write in the sound cues—this is radio, you know.** Assign each group one of the parables.

Step 3 (5-10 minutes): Reassemble the class and let groups present their script. Record each presentation. If you have time, play back the tape for students to enjoy. (In addition, keep the tape for later use. Students may enjoy hearing it at another time. Parents, too, might enjoy hearing a sample of the learning their students are doing.) Have them tell what they feel was the meaning of their parable. Correct and supplement as needed, using material from the INSIGHTS FOR THE LEADER.

Step 4 (3-5 minutes): Lead a discussion of practical ways to show care and concern for the lost.

Tell your students, **Having explored what Christ had to say about His concern for the lost, we know that Christians should share that concern.** Ask questions like these: **How can we show concern for people in our neighborhood or at school, or for other acquaintances and friends? How can we reach out to lost people we don't know? For instance, what could you do to show love to a grumpy neighbor? How could you find a way to meet a need for someone at school in order to open a door for sharing Christ?**

Conclusion and Decision

Your students may wish to see this solution to the Fun Page Puzzle.

CONCLUSION (2-3 minutes)

Tell students, **On a clean sheet of paper, write a simple instruction card that would help someone be found by Christ. Then think about someone you know who needs the card, and put the person's initials on the paper. Then decide if you would be willing to help that person be found, and indicate your answer. If you are not a Chrtistian, put your own initials and write your response to God's loving invitation to know Christ.** Students are to work individually and privately. Instruct students to save their cards as reminders.

After allowing students time to work, close in prayer. Distribute the Fun Page student take-home paper.

The Parchment

WHAT WAS LOST?

Figure it out from the word puzzle below.

SNIFF!

P + ✉ − 🪣 + Y

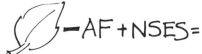

−AF + NSES =

1. What was the most valuable thing you ever lost?

2. How did you feel when you realized you had lost it?

HELP! I'M LOST!!

	Luke 15:3-7	Luke 15:8-10	Luke 15:11-32
What was lost?			
How did it get lost?			
Did it know it was lost?			
Did it know what to do?			
Who knew what to do?			
How did it become found?			
What was the result?			

LOST AND FOUND

Remember those dumb "hidden art" games you played as a child? Here's another one!

Find these objects: Lost coin (Luke 15:8-10); lost son (Luke 15:11-32); lost sheep (Luke 15:3-7); lost key; lost glasses; lost dentures; lost wig; lost cat; lost shoe; lost report card; lost marbles; lost Dutchman mine; lost continent of Atlantis; lost in space; lost lunch; lost cause.

NOTE: From "lost marbles" on: not really!

(Lost my mind.)

DAILY NUGGETS

Day 1 Read Matthew 18:12-14. Who is represented by the man, by the 99 sheep, and by the lost sheep? What does verse 14 tell you about God's character?

Day 2 Luke 15:8-10. If you've ever lost something important, how did you feel? How did you feel when you found it? How do you suppose God feels when He finds a lost son or daughter?

Day 3 Luke 15:11-32. Name some of the blessings God has given you.

Day 4 Hebrews 13:5. If both sons mentioned in Luke 15:11-31 had followed Hebrews 13:5, do you think they would have behaved as they did?

Day 5 Psalm 55:22. Memorize this verse.

Day 6 Jude 20-25. Make a list of what these verses tell us to do. Next, write what Jesus did for us.

HOT THOT

"I tell you that in the same way there will be more rejoicing in heaven over one sinner who repents than over ninety-nine righteous persons who do not need to repent."

Luke 15:7

THEME: Like the good shepherd who watched over and protected his sheep, Jesus watches over and protects us.

Session 6

BIBLE STUDY OUTLINE

Read **Psalm 23** to your students. Because the Psalm is self-explanatory, it is not necessary to add much in the way of comment. Instead, lead a discussion based on the Object Lesson and the Discussion Questions.

OBJECT LESSON: PROTECTION

Point out to your students that the main theme of Psalm 23 is protection. Say something like, **Jesus is the good Shepherd who watches over and protects us. Yes, problems and troubles still sometimes occur, but Jesus is always there to help us. I wonder how many of you realize just how important protection is to the human race. As a matter of fact, almost everything we do is somehow related to protecting ourselves. Let me show you what I mean.**

Tell your listeners that many of the things they can see in the room are designed for protection. Give them a few examples such as sweaters (protect from the cold), shoes (protect the feet from injury), and wax on the floor (protect the floor from wear). Ask the students to suggest other things they see that are designed to protect. Here are some things they may suggest: the walls, the ceiling, window curtains or blinds, air conditioning or heater, lights, clothes, door locks, fuses in the fuse box, smoke detectors.

Again remind students that the source of ultimate protection is Jesus Himself, and that anyone who commits his or her life to Christ is under His protection.

NOTES

DISCUSSION QUESTIONS

1. **Why is humanity so concerned about protection?**

2. **In what ways can Jesus protect us?**

3. **Is there anything from which He can't protect us?**

4. **Why do you think so many people fail to seek Jesus for protection?**

5. **Name as many things as you can find in Psalm 23 that are related to the idea of protection.**

THE COMPLETE
JUNIOR HIGH BIBLE STUDY
RESOURCE BOOK #3

Put those skateboards to good use. These games require a large gym with a wooden floor or a big room with indoor/outdoor carpeting.

SKATE TRAIN RACE

Line players up on skateboards as shown, three or four to a team. One member of each team pushes the skate train, and the person on the front board does his or her best to steer the team along the race course. The course should be oval. When players fall off, which happens frequently, the teams must hurriedly reassemble and continue on. The teams who usually win are those that take their time and drive carefully. To form the race track, use chairs as pylons.

SKATEBOARD WHEELBARROW RACE

Couples race together as shown.

TWO-BY-FOUR RACES

Construct a track out of two-by-fours by laying the lumber as shown. The player on the board cannot touch the ground with hands or feet. Have time trials to see who can complete the race the fastest.

A player who falls must get up and continue on.

You can nail the boards together for a more durable track, but it isn't necessary. A loose track is a lot of laughs. A track set outdoors on a grassy hill is also very fun. On a hill, riders do not need someone to push them, but they must be allowed to touch the ground with hands and/or feet.

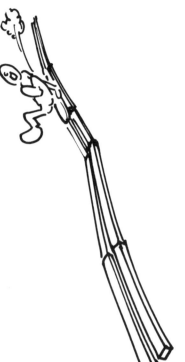

The Helping Heart

INSIGHTS FOR THE LEADER

WHAT THE SESSION IS ABOUT

Loving your neighbor means sharing his or her burden.

SCRIPTURE STUDIED

Luke 10:25-37

KEY PASSAGE

"He answered: 'Love the Lord your God with all your heart and with all your soul and with all your strength and with all your mind'; and, 'Love your neighbor as yourself.'" Luke 10:27

AIMS OF THE SESSION

During this session your learners will:
1. Tell how the Samaritan helped the man in distress;
2. Discuss how Christians can reach out to help others in distress;
3. Offer a personal plan to reach out to someone.

This session takes a look at the parable of the good Samaritan. (See Luke 10:25-37.) The central theme of the parable is the Christian's responsibility to have compassion for anyone in need. A Christian must have a helping heart.

This story is given in answer to a lawyer's question, "What must I do to inherit eternal life?" (Luke 10:25). This question was asked as a test question (see v. 25), so we don't know if the lawyer was really seeking eternal life or merely hoping to trap Jesus.

Jesus responded, not by answering the question, but by asking, "What is written in the Law? . . . How do you read it?" (Luke 10:26). Literally, Jesus was telling the lawyer to recite the Law. Like a schoolboy, this noted lawyer then quoted, "'Love the Lord your God with all your heart and with all your soul and with all your strength and with all your mind'; and, 'Love your neighbor as yourself'" (v.27). (See also Deut. 6:5; Lev. 19:18.) "'You have answered correctly,' Jesus replied. 'Do this and you will live'" (Luke 10:28).

How foolish the lawyer must have appeared to those looking on. He had answered his own question. The lawyer had been outwitted. To justify himself, he asked Jesus, "And who is my neighbor?" (v. 29). Jesus' reply is a classic tale.

The Neighbor

The story begins with a man on a journey from Jerusalem to Jericho. This is not a long journey, only 17 miles. Yet it is a rugged trail, for in the space of these few miles the road drops more than 3,000 feet from hilltop to desert floor. This twisting road was infested with robbers. The man making the journey fell victim to robbers, who stripped him and beat him, leaving him near death.

A priest happened along. We are not told if the priest was going to, or coming from, Jerusalem. If he was going to Jerusalem, he may have been going to serve at the Temple. If this were the case, it was necessary to keep himself ceremonially clean. Levitical law required that a person who touched anything unclean was to be considered unclean for seven days and must twice go through a purifying ceremony of washing. (See Num. 19:11,12). If he had touched anything unclean, the priest would have been unable to take part in his priestly function. But we are not told if this was the case. We are only told that he did not take the time to see if the traveler was dead or alive. He just passed on by, moving to the other side of the road.

Some time later, a Levite came by. The Levite, like the priest, was part of the religious leadership. Though Levites did not have quite the same high place as the priests, they were still important men who were responsible for

NOTES

the Temple liturgy and policing the Temple grounds.

This man also passed the injured man right by. Was his excuse fear? Was he frightened that this man was a decoy, setting him up for ambush? Was he afraid of being beaten and robbed? We don't know. Yet both men, part of the religious upper crust, passed by. They did not care enough about their fellow man to interrupt their journeys. They did not love their brother.

The third traveler on the scene was a Samaritan. For 400 years the Jews and Samaritans had been fighting. The story goes back to the fall of the Jewish Northern Kingdom in 722 B.C. From that time on the defeated Jews had intermarried with foreigners. They lost their racial purity. They also changed their center of worship from Jerusalem to Samaria. These mixed Jews were the Samaritans. In 440 B.C., when Ezra and Nehemiah began to rebuild the city of Jerusalem and the Temple, the Samaritans offered their help. It was refused, rudely. Naturally, this promoted bitter hatred between the Jews and the Samaritans.

And yet, in Jesus' story it was the Samaritan who was moved by pity and came to the aid of the wounded man (presumably a Jew). He treated the wounds with wine as a disinfectant and oil to soothe the pain. Note that these must have been his own oil and wine. He may have had other plans for them, but he willingly gave them up in order to help the victim.

After rendering first aid, the Samaritan placed the injured man on his own donkey and took him to an inn. Since the wounded man was penniless, having been robbed, the Samaritan made advance payment to the innkeeper to care for him. Thus we have seen in how many ways the Samaritan helped the man in distress.

Now Jesus asked those around him, "Which of these three do you think was a neighbor?" (Luke 10:36). There was only one possible answer: "The one who had mercy on him" (v.37).

James wrote: "What good is it, my brothers, if a man claims to have faith but has no deeds? Can such faith save him? Suppose a brother or sister is without clothes and daily food. If one of you says to him, 'Go, I wish you well; keep warm and well fed,' but does nothing about his physical needs, what good is it? In the same way, faith by itself, if it is not accompanied by action, is dead" (Jas. 2:14-17).

Being Neighborly

Jesus said much the same thing. He tells us that when we provide food, drink or clothing, or when we care for or visit someone, we are doing it for Him. (See Matt. 25:34-40.) Jesus' teaching is clear. We must have mercy on those in need. We must have pity on them. Our compassion and faith must produce ministry to others less fortunate. We must possess a helping heart.

Your students will frequently find themselves in the same position as the priest, the Levite and the Samaritan of this story. Someone around them will be less fortunate or in need of help. They must then decide how they will respond to the individual in need. Will they be like the priest, afraid to become unclean? Is the other person too different? Are they fearful of becoming associated with someone "like that"? Are they afraid of what others will think if they are seen with a needy person? Or are they like the Levite, concerned that the person needing aid is a trap to lure them away from their possessions or friends by demanding too much of their time?

Jesus declares that we are to be a true neighbor to all in need. We are to emulate the Samaritan, offering our love, time, money and concern to any who need us. Junior highers can be loving neighbors by befriending a lonesome young person, sharing possessions, baby-sitting for someone who cannot afford it, mowing a lawn or cleaning house for an elderly or sick person. They, too, need to possess a helping heart!

SESSION PLAN

BEFORE CLASS BEGINS: Photocopy enough Parchment worksheets for each student to have one.

Attention Grabber

ATTENTION GRABBER (2-3 minutes)

When students have all arrived, ask them, **If you saw a man lying in the gutter, beaten and bloody and obviously in need of help, what would you do?** Most of your learners will probably say that they would help him, or phone the police for help. Ask, **What are some reasons you might turn away without offering help? What would scare you away?** Allow students to speak.

Make a transition to the next part of the session by saying, **Today we're going to read the parable that is the source of the expression "good Samaritan." The surprising thing about this story is that some good people turned away from a man in desperate need.**

Bible Exploration

EXPLORATION (25-30 minutes)

Step 1 (10-12 minutes): Distribute the Parchment worksheets. Instruct students to work in pairs or individually to complete the "Samaritan Crosswords" puzzle. (It is best if students use the NIV or NASB versions of the Bible.)

Step 2 (5-6 minutes): Allow students 10-12 minutes to complete their puzzles, then begin a discussion of what they have learned. Correct any inaccurate ideas and add information as needed,

NOTES

using the material in the INSIGHTS FOR THE LEADER.

Step 3 (10-12 minutes): On your chalkboard, write the following three headings: "What's Yours Is Mine;" "What's Mine Is Mine;" and "What's Mine Is Yours."

Now ask your students, **Which heading describes the attitude of the robbers?** Allow students to respond, and then say something like, **The robbers' attitude is described by the heading, "What's Yours Is Mine." They beat the victim up, robbed him and left him to die because they wanted what he had. This is a completely selfish attitude toward life. Anyone who thinks only of himself and how he can get others to do things for him or how he can get things from them holds the same basic outlook on life.**

Ask your students, **Which heading describes the attitude of the priest and Levite?** The priest and the Levite represent the second attitude: "What's Mine Is Mine." Say, **We can almost hear the priest and Levite saying, "What's mine is mine—I'm going to keep it." These men passed by the wounded man without offering to help. Perhaps they were too busy, or feared the consequences of involvement. This, too,** is a selfish outlook on life. This sort of person is concerned only about himself. Though he would not steal from others, neither would he give to help others, no matter how needy they may be.

The third attitude is illustrated by the Samaritan: "What's mine is yours—I'll share it!" He could have passed by like the priest and the Levite. He could have excused himself because of the possible danger and because of the racial differences. But he didn't pass by. His outlook on life was based on love and on caring for others, so he stopped and got involved. It cost him time, effort and money. This is the selfless attitude, the opposite of selfishness. This sort of person thinks first of the needs of others.

Ask, **How would you recognize a good Samaritan if you saw one today? What would a good Samaritan be doing (a) in your neighborhood, (b) at your school, (c) in your home?**

Make a transition to the Conclusion by saying, **You've given us some good ideas here for things a good Samaritan would be doing. Now you'll have an opportunity to decide what you will do.**

Conclusion and Decision

CONCLUSION (3-5 minutes)

Instruct students to individually complete the "What Can I Do?" portion of the Parchment worksheet. Allow 3 to 5 minutes, then close in prayer. Distribute the Fun Page student take-home paper.

Note: Special preparation two or three days before class meets is required for the next session, session 8. See "BEFORE CLASS BEGINS" on page 90.

Samaritan Crosswords

This crossword puzzle is based on the story Jesus told about the good Samaritan. You'll find it in Luke 10:25-37.

ACROSS

1. In verse 30, a what was going to Jericho?
2. The coins were made out of (v. 35).
4. In verse 30, the man was going down _____ Jerusalem.
9. Verse 27 hints that God should be our what?
10. One of the things we are to love God with (verse 27).
11. The man _____ on top of the donkey.
12. The man was left half what?
13. The expert wanted what kind of life?
16. The robbers _____ the man half dead.
18. Abbreviation for "Medical Doctor"—what the wounded man needed!
20. One of the things we are to love God with.
22. Who are we to love as ourselves?
23. The expert stood up to do what to Jesus?
28. One of the things the Samaritan poured on the man.
29. The expert wanted to do this with eternal life.
30. The place the man was heading to.
31. In verse 37, what the Samaritan had on the man.
33. The Samaritan left the man with whom?
35. Another thing we are to love God with.
36. This man who tested Jesus was an _____ in the law.

DOWN

1. A thing we are to love God with (verse 27).
2. The priest and Levite passed the man on the other _____ of the road.
3. We are to do what to God in verse 27?
4. The man did what into the hands of the robbers?
5. The expert wanted to know what he _____ do to inherit eternal life.
6. The Samaritan took what on the man (verse 33)?
7. The Lord our _____.
8. The robbers may have said, "This is a _____ up!"
9. The expert was an expert in what field?
10. What nationality was the good man?
14. Another word for "robber" or "goon."
15. The man was left half dead by whom?
17. Short for "fortress"—what the man could have used!
19. The priest and who else passed the injured man?
21. The expert addressed Jesus as what?
24. How many coins the Samaritan gave the innkeeper.
25. What did the Samaritan bandage?
26. Another word for "everything" (see verse 27).
27. This man and the Levite passed the injured man.
31. One of the Three Stooges.
32. Another word for "wound."
33. Frozen water (sometimes good for wounds).
34. A short rest (probably just what the wounded man needed).

What Can I Do?

In a few words, list some nice things you could do for these people:

- Best friend
- Family member
- A new kid in school

Now choose one nice thing you actually will do this week.

IT'S BEEN A BAD DAY FOR GOOD SAMARITANS!

Remember the story of the good Samaritan (Luke 10:30-37)? The Samaritan man found an injured Jewish man on the road and kindly helped him back to health. Well, now the Jewish man wants to return the favor!

Help him pick up as many injured Samaritans as he can. Start down in the bottom left corner and find the route with the most Samaritans. End up in Jericho at the top.

There are two important rules: 1. You cannot use the same section of path twice, not even for a fraction of an inch.
2. You cannot cross your own path except with one of the bridges.

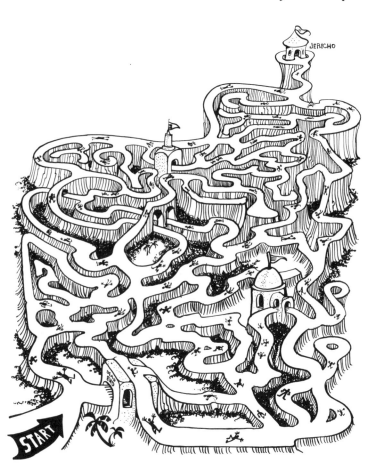

JERICHO

START

DAILY NUGGETS

Day 1 Read Matthew 5:43-48. Why do you suppose God wants us to love our enemies?

Day 2 Leviticus 19:18; Mark 12:30,31. What two commandments are God's most important?

Day 3 Luke 6:27-36. Is there someone you can reach out to that hasn't been treating you kindly?

Day 4 Romans 12:9-19. If someone does you wrong, what should your attitude be?

Day 5 Galatians 5:13. What does our freedom in Christ give us an opportunity to do? What is one way you could serve another person in love this week?

Day 6 Ephesians 4:2,3. How will you respond to a friend who makes a lot of mistakes?

HOT-THOT

"He answered: 'Love the Lord your God with all your heart and with all your soul and with all your strength and with all your mind'; and, 'Love your neighbor as yourself.'"

Luke 10:27

Samaritan score:

44—LOUSY!
45—DO IT AGAIN!
46—NOT BAD
50—GOOD
52—EXCELLENT
53—GENIUS
      OR CHEATER!

THEME: The royal law.

Session 7

BIBLE STUDY OUTLINE

Read James 2:1-9 to your students, stressing these points as time allows:

- VERSE 1: As Christians, we are not to show favoritism. Favoritism is a common sin, and usually has an evil motive. We tend to favor people who we think can help us or from whom we can get something. Many times we don't really care about the people we favor, we are just "buttering them up."
- VERSES 2-4: James now gives us an example of favoritism. This particular example may apply to adults more than to people your age, but the principle applies to everyone. You may not show favor to rich kids, but I bet many of you tend to be more friendly to good-looking, talented or athletically-skilled people than to ugly, stupid or socially-inept people. It's natural to show that sort of favoritism. And it's a sin.
- VERSE 5: This verse indicates that God often looks at people differently than we do. God values the poor people, even if we humans tend to ignore them. And we can be sure that God also values the ugly, stupid and socially inept. He loves them. As children of God, we Christians also must show love and acceptance toward them.

  It's not always easy to be friendly and accepting to oddballs and unpopular people. But Christ expects us to set an example of love. God's love is meant to be shared and given away.
- VERSES 8,9: "Love your neighbor as yourself" is called the royal law because it is the supreme law. It's the chief rule of Christian life, along with the commandment to love God. We cannot be selective with this law. We can't choose to love a few people and ignore the rest, for that is favoritism. As we have opportunity, we are to care for all people—rich, poor, smart, dumb, cool or clod.

OBJECT LESSON: THE SIGN

Bring a road sign, poster, or one or more bumper stickers to class. Tell your listeners that a sign, poster or bumper sticker always communicates some sort of message. Say, **The message may be "wet paint" or "yield" or anything else. Love—the sort of love that James speaks of—is also a sign. A person who loves his neighbor as himself is sending a message. The message says, "God is real and at work in me and through me." Love is our sign. God's love working through us is what tells the world that God is real.**

If you wish, you may show your students a faded or defaced sign and talk about Christians who aren't properly displaying their "sign."

DISCUSSION QUESTIONS

1. **What is favoritism? What are some common ways people your age show favoritism?**

2. **What are some reasons people show favoritism?**

3. **Why do you suppose favoritism is so wrong in God's eyes?**

4. **When God says we are to love our neighbor, does that mean we necessarily have to feel an emotional high for everyone we meet? What is the difference between the love of God that we are to demonstrate and emotional or romantic love?**

5. **What are some practical ways to show God's love to people you know?**

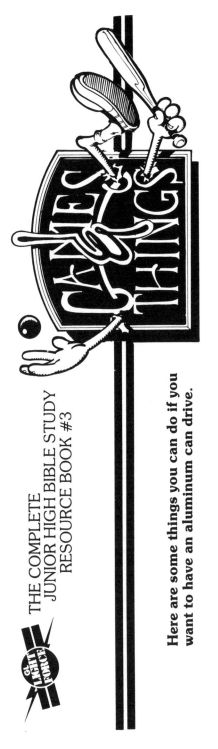

THE COMPLETE
JUNIOR HIGH BIBLE STUDY
RESOURCE BOOK #3

Here are some things you can do if you want to have an aluminum can drive.

CAN DO

By setting cans one at a time beneath a player lying on the floor, teams try to be the first to raise a player completely off the ground. The player being raised, however, belongs to one of the opposing teams. He or she can resist being elevated, but only by acting like a dead weight. The player cannot squirm or otherwise intentionally knock over a can. When the player can no longer touch the ground with any part of his or her body, that team has finished the race. Teams should be small; three to five players each.

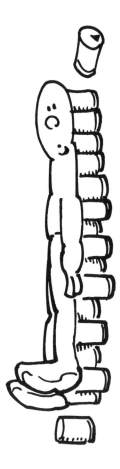

CAN SQUASH

Set an equal number of cans in two large areas (fifty cans or so each). At the signal, two teams race into their areas and start crushing cans with their feet. Great way to get a lot of cans squashed in a hurry.

CAN-IVAL GAMES

Here are several simple suggestions for games played with cans:

1. Have a western-style shootout with dart guns and cans lined up as targets.

2. Fill a large trash can with aluminum cans. Place a candy bar or other small prize in the can. Give each contestant three seconds to reach in and try to find the prize.

3. Play broom hockey or soccer with a can.

4. Throw baseballs at a stack of cans. Or, using a larger ball, play a game of bowling with ten cans set as bowling pins.

The Forgiving Heart

INSIGHTS FOR THE LEADER

WHAT THE SESSION IS ABOUT

We must forgive other people's sins as Jesus forgave ours.

SCRIPTURE STUDIED

Matthew 18:21-35

KEY PASSAGE

"Be kind and compassionate to one another, forgiving each other, just as in Christ God forgave you."
Ephesians 4:32

AIMS OF THE SESSION

During this session your learners will:

1. Explain Jesus' teaching on forgiveness;
2. Discuss the importance of forgiving others;
3. Be challenged to talk to God about a forgiving spirit.

In this session you and your students will be looking at forgiveness in the parable of the unforgiving servant (see Matt. 18:21-35). The biblical principle described is: If we don't forgive others, then we go unforgiven by God (see Matt. 6:14,15). A forgiving heart is essential to the Christian life. Peter came to Jesus saying, "Lord, how many times shall I forgive my brother when he sins against me?" (Matt. 18:21).

A Lot of Times, Anyway

Peter had even calculated what he thought was a generous answer, seven times. The rabbis taught that a person only needed to forgive someone three times. Peter had more than doubled that number. Yet Jesus' response was to take Peter's seven and multiply it. (The Greek at this point is somewhat ambiguous; it could be translated "seventy plus seven," [77].) Bible translators differ on which is the correct number and have written their translations accordingly.) Whether Jesus said that Peter was to forgive his brother 490 times or 77, the number is so large that it would be hard to remember that many offenses. Jesus was really saying that His followers shouldn't even keep a record of those who offend, but should simply forgive.

The Parable of the Unfaithful Servant

To illustrate His point, Jesus told the disciples a parable on forgiveness. This parable is about "the kingdom of heaven" (Matt. 18:23). Thus, we are looking at the forgiveness of God in this story.

The king in the story wanted to balance his books. As he began, he discovered that a man owed him 10,000 talents. This was a huge amount, the equivalent of millions of dollars. The man who owed this debt had nothing. He was broke. The king commanded that the man, his wife and children, and all their possessions should be sold in order to repay the debt. The man would lose his belongings, his family and his freedom in one disastrous stroke.

The debt was so large, the man was bankrupt; there was no hope except for the mercy of the king. "The servant fell on his knees before him. 'Be patient with me,' he begged, 'and I will pay back everything'" (v. 26). The servant threw himself on the mercy of the king, and the king "took pity on him, canceled the debt and let him go" (v. 27). The total amount was forgiven. It was marked, "Paid in full." In the same way, our debts have been paid by the blood of Jesus. We are forgiven, "As far as the east is from the west, so far has he removed our transgressions from us" (Ps. 103:12).

This servant was forgiven, but he had not learned anything about forgiveness. He had not taken a lesson from the merciful king. A fel-

NOTES

low servant owed him the sum of one hundred denarii. One denarius was the standard day's wage of an average man. It took 6,000 denarii to equal one talent. This man had been forgiven a debt of 10,000 talents or 60 million denarii. Yet he attacked the man who owed him one-six-hundred-thousandth that amount.

To help your students visualize the difference between the two amounts, use the following amounts on the chalkboard: 60,000,000 vs. 100.

"Pay up!" the first servant screamed as he choked the other man (see Matt. 18:28). The debtor "fell to his knees and begged him, 'Be patient with me, and I will pay you back'" (v. 29). But there was no forgiveness in the servant's heart. He had the debtor thrown into prison.

The servant's merciless behavior distressed those who saw the incident. Out of their concern they went to the king. The king's servant was wicked because he held an unforgiving spirit. He had been forgiven a vast amount, but he would not forgive a much smaller debt. The king's sentence was just: He "turned him over to the jailers to be tortured, until he should pay back all he owed" (v. 34).

Since God forgives and forgets our sins, we must forgive others. Jesus said, "For if you forgive men when they sin against you, your heavenly Father will also forgive you. But if you do not forgive men their sins, your Father will not forgive your sins" (Matt. 6:14,15).

Three Important Steps

Christians must forgive others, but this is hard to do. We really cannot do it without God's help. If we are going to forgive others, first we must recognize the extent to which God went in order to forgive us.

The next step is to pray for strength to forgive others. Jesus instructs us, "Love your enemies and pray for those who persecute you" (Matt. 5:44). We need His help to be able to do that.

The third step is to ask for God to heal the hurt caused by those we forgive. Forgiveness is an act of the will that adults and young people can choose to make. But feelings are not so easy to control. Again, God is the only real source of hope.

SESSION PLAN

BEFORE CLASS BEGINS: The ATTENTION GRABBER requires a container of milk that you have allowed to spoil. Set out a small amount of milk in a plastic container with a tight-fitting lid. Let it remain at room temperature for two or three days before your class meets so that it will be thoroughly spoiled and smelly, in order to make the maximum impact. Also, cut out the "Folded Questions" on the Teaching Resource page (which follows the Parchment worksheet) and photocopy enough Parchments for each student to have one. You need a hat or other container to hold the "Folded Questions."

Attention Grabber

ATTENTION GRABBER (2-3 minutes)

Materials needed: A small container of milk which you have allowed to spoil.

Pass the container of spoiled milk around the class and let students take a whiff of it. Then guide a discussion using the following suggestions: Ask, **Why does this milk smell so bad?** (It has spoiled and become rotten.) **What causes it to be rotten?** (Microorganisms have attacked it and are breaking it down.) **What would have prevented it from smelling so bad?** (It could have been preserved by canning, freezing, or refrigerating.)

Make a transition to the EXPLORATION by saying something like this: **Our session today has to do with forgiveness. Holding grudges against people, failing to forgive them, is an attitude that will produce in your life the same sort of spiritual odor that was produced in this milk when I let it spoil. Your anger, resentment or complaining will drive people away as this rotting odor does. If you don't want that kind of stink in your life, you need to learn from the Lord how to forgive. This session should help get you started in that learning process.**

Bible Exploration

EXPLORATION (20-30 minutes)

Materials needed: A hat or box to contain the "Folded Questions" from the Teaching Resource page.

Step 1 (10-15 minutes): Distribute the Parchment student worksheets. Read Matthew 18:21-35 to the class (or have several volunteers read portions). Lead a class discussion based on the "Keeping the Ledger" section of the Parchment. Fill in additional information as needed, using material from the INSIGHTS FOR THE LEADER. Make sure students understand the enormous difference between the amounts owed by the two servants.

Step 2 (3-5 minutes): Have students form groups of two to four. Go from group to group with the "Folded Questions" from the Teaching Resource page in a hat or cardboard box, and let each group draw one question. Then tell them, **Unfold and read your question. Then discuss it together until you arrive at an answer to share with the class.** (For a small class, give questions to individuals.)

Step 3 (5-10 minutes): Reassemble the class and have each group read its question and tell its answer. Guide a brief discussion of the importance of forgiveness. Use material from INSIGHTS FOR THE LEADER for this discussion. Also bring in the ideas from the end of INSIGHTS FOR THE LEADER about the three steps of forgiving others. Stress the fact that forgiveness is a *choice*, an act of the will. It may take time for the feelings of anger and hurt to subside, but with God's help they should do so after the choice to forgive is made.

NOTES

During your discussion, ask your class to brainstorm ways to be able to forgive. Ideas may include:

Praying for the person.

Asking God to help in forgiving.

Talking about your feelings with someone you trust.

Thinking of a kind act to do for the other person, then actually doing it.

Asking the other person to forgive you for your unforgiving attitude.

Then give a brief wrap-up by saying something like the following: **You've given an interesting list of ways to be able to forgive. It's very human and normal to find it hard to forgive when people do terrible things. But God would forgive all those sins; in fact, He has forgiven them by Christ's death on the cross. And He wants to help us forgive, too. He doesn't want us to suffer from the rottenness of an unforgiving spirit in our lives. He wants us to enjoy the clean, fresh, wholesome spirit of forgiveness that He offers.**

Conclusion and Decision

CONCLUSION (3-5 minutes)

Tell students, **Use a blank sheet of paper to write a letter asking someone to forgive you, or forgiving someone against whom you have been holding a grudge. You can decide whether you want to mail your letter or tear it up later.**

After allowing time for students to write, close in prayer.

Distribute the Fun Page as students leave.

Note: Session 9, the next session, requires a certificate of ownership for a car or boat. See "BEFORE CLASS BEGINS," page 103 for details.

The Parchment

Keeping the Ledger

Read Matthew 18:21-35. As you discuss these questions, fill in the answers.

Servant #1

- How much did he owe?

- Converted to denarii, how much was that? (Talents × 6000 = denarii.)

- What was the king's initial judgment against this servant?

- What did the servant ask for?

- How did the king respond?

- Why do you think the king did that?

Servant #2

- How much did he owe?

- How did servant #1 treat him when they met?

- What did servant #2 ask for?

- What did servant #1 respond?

- Why do you think he did that?

Tell in your own words what happened after the first servant had the second servant thrown in jail:

- Why did the king change his mind about his treatment of the first servant?

- What did the king do?

- What point do you think Jesus was making with this story?

- How many times should we be willing to forgive, according to verses 21,22?

- Why?

Bible Coin Exchange

1 talent = 6,000 denarii

1 denarius = 6 one day's wages for a common laborer

Therefore 1 talent = 6,000 days' wages or nearly 16½ YEARS of work.

How many years of work does 10,000 talents represent?

Folded Questions

Cut apart these questions, fold them and place them in a hat or other container for students to draw out and discuss.

Question 1
What do you think this parable says about carrying a grudge against a person?

Question 5
What's the difference between forgiving and forgetting?

Question 2
Compare Matthew 6:12,14,15 with the story studied. What impresses you with these verses?

Question 6
"My forgiving others is a measure of my gratefulness to God for forgiving me." Do you agree or disagree? Tell why.

Question 3
What does it mean to forgive someone? Explain.

Question 7
"That's so little to forgive when I think of how much God has forgiven me." What do you think of a statement like that?

Question 4
How should you treat someone you have forgiven? Explain why.

WE DROPPED IT AND BROKE IT!

Cut up and put it back together.

DAILY NUGGETS
Wisdom from God's Word for you to read each day.

Day 1 Read Matthew 18:21,22. Forgiving someone 490 times is a lot of times. What point do you think Jesus is making?

Day 2 Mark 11:25. Is there someone you need to forgive before you start praying?

Day 3 Romans 12:14-21. Write down the things we are to do and the things we are not to do. How can we take action against evil?

Day 4 1 John 1:9. What two things does God do when we confess our sins?

Day 5 Matthew 6:9-15. Jesus taught us a way to pray. As we forgive others, what does the Father do for us?

Day 6 Ephesians 4:32; Colossians 3:13. Who is our model for forgiveness? What attitudes should we hold toward those we need to forgive?

"Be kind and compassionate to one another, forgiving each other, just as in Christ God forgave you."
Ephesians 4:32

THE COMPLETE JUNIOR HIGH BIBLE STUDY RESOURCE BOOK #3
© 1988 GL/LIGHT FORCE, VENTURA, CA 93006

THEME: We must forgive others as Jesus forgave us.

BIBLE STUDY OUTLINE

Read Romans 12:14-21 and make the following remarks as time permits.

- VERSE 14: This passage in Romans speaks about the incredible style of life that Christians are supposed to live. It is incredible because it is so radically opposed to the usual way people behave. Take verse 14 for example. It says that believers are to bless people who cause them trouble—that's the exact opposite of what our human nature wants to do. We want to strike out at those who strike at us. We want to hurt those who hurt us. But God says that Christians are to be different. They are to do good to those who are against them.
- VERSE 15: When somebody rejoices or mourns, the Christian is supposed to feel what that person feels and be with him or her for support—even if it's someone who opposes the believer.
- VERSE 16: And Christians are to associate with people who are labeled as lowly or losers. Again, it's human nature to avoid the oddball or peculiar person. But God says to go out of your way to associate with each of them. That's exactly what Christ did when He walked this planet, and now those who follow Him are to do it.
- VERSE 17: Christians are warned not to repay wrong for wrong. And they are to make a special effort always to do the right things. These all seem like hard demands, but no one ever said it's easy to be a Christian.
- VERSE 18: This verse speaks of peace. Peace means agreement, friendship, calmness and tranquillity. Humanly speaking, it is very difficult to have that sort of relationship with everyone. But believers in Christ are to make the effort, and with God's help, can enjoy peace with those around them.
- VERSE 19: It's nice to know that this passage isn't telling Christians to just roll over and let everyone use them as doormats. On the contrary, this verse reminds believers that God is very much interested in the way they are treated, and He will eventually balance the scales if they are mistreated. Remember, though, that it is God who repays. The Christian's job is to do what the rest of the passage says to do.
- VERSE 20: Here's an interesting insight into human nature: doing good for someone who hates you will drive them crazy! Perhaps some of you have been kind to an acquaintance who dislikes you. If so, you've probably noticed that the person either goes away and leaves you alone, or becomes your best friend! People don't expect to be treated nicely—it takes them by surprise.
- VERSE 21: Finally, overcome evil with good. Kindness is the only permanent solution to meanness.

These verses teach true wisdom to live by. If you want to follow Christ, take these verses to your heart. Put them into action. Christianity is an *action* faith. God doesn't want us to just sit around thinking spiritual thoughts—He wants us to put that spirituality "on the road" where it can make a real difference in those we meet.

OBJECT LESSON: THE KNIFE

Bring a knife to show, the meaner and uglier the better. Say something like, **Knives are often the symbol of how we treat our enemies. We speak of "stabbing someone in the back" or "staring knives" at someone, or even "cutting remarks." But we Christians must put the knives away. God calls us to be peacemakers.**

DISCUSSION QUESTIONS

1. **How do you suppose most people would react to a kindness returned for a hurtful remark or action? How do you think this world would be different if everyone followed the wisdom in this Scripture passage?**

2. **Why is it sometimes difficult for people to "Rejoice with those who rejoice; mourn with those who mourn," as it says in verse 15?**

3. **Why do you think we are warned against conceit in verse 16?**

4. **What do you feel are some of the advantages and rewards of following the wisdom we've read?**

Mystery Games

A change of pace from our usual action games. These mystery guessing games make wonderful time-wasters on long trips or slow afternoons. Here's how they work: You tell your kids the mystery, their job is to guess the solution. In finding the solution, the kids can ask you questions that can be answered "yes," "no," or "not important."

On the first mystery, for example, a person might ask, "Was the light bulb in the room burned out?" The answer is no. The next question could be, "Was the electricity out?" The answer is no. By asking as many questions as necessary, the players will eventually arrive at the answer. These mystery games can last a half hour or longer. If you wish, you can cut down the time by dropping a few simple hints.

THE JANITOR

Mystery: The janitor flipped on the wall switch, but the lights in the darkened room didn't come on. When he sat down, he never got up again. Why?

Answer: The janitor worked at a prison. He sat down in an electric chair which he had accidentally switched on.

THE DOCTOR

This mystery seems easy to solve. But you will probably find that it confounds a lot of kids!

Mystery: A man and his son were in a serious car accident. When they arrived at the hospital, the doctor said, "I can't operate on the child, he's my son." How is this possible?

Answer: The doctor was the son's mother.

THE WIFE

Mystery: The murdered woman was lying dead on the floor. The room was empty except for a large raw beef steak draped over her face. The police arrested her husband the butcher, and claimed that the steak was the murder weapon. How was she killed?

Answer: The husband hit her on the head with the steak when it was frozen.

The Selfish Spirit

INSIGHTS FOR THE LEADER

WHAT THE SESSION IS ABOUT

In order to have a rich relationship with God, we must put our trust in Him.

SCRIPTURE STUDIED

Luke 12:15-21

KEY PASSAGE

"Then he said to them, 'Watch out! Be on your guard against all kinds of greed; a man's life does not consist in the abundance of his possessions.'" Luke 12:15

AIMS OF THE SESSION

During this session your learners will:

1. Discuss the story of the rich fool;
2. Explore ways a person can have a better relationship with God;
3. Examine their personal spiritual investments.

In today's lesson on the parable of the rich fool (see Luke 12:16-21) we see a man possessed by possessions. The theme of the parable is temporal riches compared to eternal riches. The man in the story found his riches in the abundance of possessions. He was secure in the ownership of land and vast storage barns. His pleasure was in taking life easy, dining and drinking and having a good time. He thought that he had the world by the tail. Life was for his pleasure and pleasure was for his life.

Yet true wealth is trust in God. True riches mean serving the Lord. Christians have not always realized this truth. The church at Laodicea failed to recognize this fact. The church said, "I am rich; I have acquired wealth and do not need a thing" (Rev. 3:17). But Jesus said, "You do not realize that you are wretched, pitiful, poor, blind and naked" (Rev. 3:17). He also said that He would spit them out of His mouth. (See Rev. 3:16.) Evidently the lukewarm attitude of the Laodiceans was disgusting to Him. They had not learned that true riches are found not in possessions but in surrendering our lives to God and serving Him.

Greed

At the beginning of today's Scripture Jesus was asked to settle a dispute over inheritance. Jesus did not get involved in the dispute, perhaps because the Old Testament clearly taught that the eldest male received two-thirds of the inheritance (see Deut. 21:15-17). Biblical scholars indicate that younger sons, by custom, shared equally in the remaining property. Thus, there was most likely no real question for Jesus to answer. The law and established custom were sufficient. But Jesus used the opportunity to go to the core of the dispute—greed. He taught about that which has real value. He taught that the man who is rich in regard to God is truly rich (see Luke 12:21).

Jesus told of a foolish man whose security was in what he owned in real estate and grain. His land was so productive that he did not have room to store all his crops, so he decided to build larger barns. All he was concerned with was himself and what he could do to make himself richer. He was investing all of his time and all of his resources on the "now." He did not spend a second or a penny on the hereafter. All he could see was this world and its goods. He was a pure materialist. He was blind to eternity. He was deaf to God. He was unconcerned for others. He cared only about full barns and acquiring more goods. He had not considered the future and the death it must surely hold. All his riches could not add a single second to his life. All his wealth could not keep death from him.

God said to him, "You fool! This very night your life will be demanded from you" (v. 20). All his life had been spent trying to amass

NOTES

wealth. Yet once he had it, he could only leave it to another.

Silver and gold are not our ultimate security. God is! Jesus said that we should bank in heaven, where our wealth won't decrease in value or be stolen. He also said that where our wealth is, there our hearts are also (see Matt. 6:21). Jesus went on to state that we should not worry about the necessities of life, like what we are to eat or what clothes to wear. Life ultimately depends upon God and His Word. If we seek God's kingdom, we need not worry about these things (see Luke 12:22-31).

Giving

The early Christians were not interested in amassing great wealth, but rather in living fully for God. At one point, when the apostles Peter and John were asked for money by a crippled beggar, Peter said, "Silver or gold I do not have, but what I have I give you. In the name of Jesus Christ of Nazareth, walk" (Acts 3:6). Though they had the power to work miracles of healing, the apostles at that point had no money.

The early church went through a stage in which those who had possessions gave them totally to the apostles to use for the ministry to the whole body of believers. "All the believers were one in heart and mind. No one claimed that any of his possessions was his own, but they shared everything they had" (Acts 4:32).

Another way in which early believers served the Lord with their possessions was by making them available for the use of the body of believers. Thus a number of believers was gathered to pray at the house of Mary the mother of John Mark the night Peter was miraculously released from prison (see Acts 12:12). Lydia, upon her conversion and baptism, invited Paul and his traveling companions to stay in her home (see Acts 16:13-15). In Rome a church body met in the home of Priscilla and Aquila (see Rom. 16:3-5).

Thus, whether by giving up their possessions entirely or by permitting them to be used by the church people, the early Christians demonstrated that things were not their primary interest.

Our ultimate aim in life is not to make a living, but to serve God. It is not impossible for a rich man to enter the kingdom of God, but it is hard (see Matt. 19:24-26). We have a tendency not to trust God for things we can acquire ourselves. Wealthy people surround themselves with many of life's necessities, including friendship, entertainment and other diversions which often cloud their real inner needs.

The New Testament provides examples of wealthy followers of Christ, such as Zacchaeus, Joseph of Arimathea and Lydia. But "from everyone who has been given much, much will be demanded" (Luke 12:48). Paul wrote to Timothy, "Command those who are rich in this present world not to be arrogant nor to put their hope in wealth, which is so uncertain, but to put their hope in God, who richly provides us with everything for our enjoyment. Command them to do good, to be rich in good deeds, and to be generous and willing to share. In this way they will lay up treasure for themselves as a firm foundation for the coming age, so that they may take hold of the life that is truly life" (1 Tim. 6:17-19).

The parable of the rich fool can have real importance in the lives of your students. Too often (especially in our affluent society) the junior higher's main concern is to own the right kind of clothes or the best stereo components, to have the most popular brand of sports equipment, to be invited to the right party on Friday night by the right person, or to enjoy any other portion of the "eat, drink and be merry" routine. But, like the rich fool of Jesus' parable, your students will not find lasting happiness in the abundance of their possessions, nor in the pleasures of the day. God tells us to store up riches in Him. The way to be rich in the Lord is to know Him, study His Word, talk with Him regularly and try to live as He would have us live. When we invest our lives in the areas that are important to God, such as being generous, sharing, doing good deeds as Paul commanded Timothy, we will be making a true spiritual investment, storing up riches in heaven!

SESSION PLAN

BEFORE CLASS BEGINS: Obtain a certificate of ownership for a car or boat (see the ATTENTION GRABBER for details). Photocopy enough Parchment worksheets for each student to have one.

Attention Grabber

ATTENTION GRABBER (1 minute)

Materials needed: Certificate of ownership for a car or boat.

Display the certificate of ownership for a car or boat and ask, **What is this?** A certificate of ownership. **What does it mean?** It means that the person named on it is the legal owner of the car or boat identified on the certificate. **If someone tried to take my car away, could they do so legally?** Not if you have the certificate of ownership to demonstrate that you are the legal owner. **Suppose your parents buy a car. They borrow money from the bank to buy it, so that bank keeps the certificate of ownership until the loan is paid. Whose car is it?** It's really the bank's until the loan is paid.

Make a transition to the next part of the session by saying, **Who has the certificate of ownership for your soul? Don't answer out loud, just think about it while we take a look at a story Jesus told—a story about a man who made the tragic mistake of thinking he owned his own soul.**

Bible Exploration

EXPLORATION (25-35 minutes)

Step 1 (5-7 minutes): Have students form groups of four to six, with a teacher in each group. (Or, if your department is not structured to allow for this, keep students together for the discussion.) Have a good reader read Luke 12:15-21 aloud while other members follow in their own Bibles. Groups should then discuss the parable, using questions like these: "How did the rich fool go wrong?" He thought he was in control. He didn't take God into account. "How can a person be rich toward God?" Making

103

sure he knows God; spending time with God; reading His Word; putting God first when deciding priorities. "What could the rich fool have done instead of building barns?" (This calls for personal opinion, but he could have shared some of his wealth with the needy rather than figuring out new ways to store it.)

Step 2 (5-7 minutes): Tell students to turn to the section of the Parchment which calls for them to write an obituary for the rich fool. Read the instructions from that section and let students work on their obituaries individually.

Step 3 (5-7 minutes): Reassemble the class and have a representative of each group report the group's responses to the discussion in Step 1; call for a few volunteers to read their obituaries from Step 2. Using material from the INSIGHTS FOR THE LEADER, add any further information needed regarding the parable of the rich fool. (Do not go into the application of the parable, as students will consider that in the next steps.)

Step 4 (3-5 minutes): Have students return to their groups and discuss the following questions (or lead a discussion with the entire class): "What does the parable say to us today?" God is more important than wealth; greed can interfere with

finding the full life that God offers. "What kind of attitude do you think God wants us to have toward temporary things such as money, beauty, fame?" While these have their place in a person's life, they are not to be the primary priority. God must be first, then other things will take their proper place.

Step 5 (5-7 minutes): Have students work individually to write an obituary for themselves, using the designated section of the Parchment. Do not ask them to share these obituaries.

ALTERNATIVE TO STEP 5: Give students sheets of poster board and felt pens. Instruct them, **Work individually or in pairs to make a poster with a motto to live by, based on what you have learned in this lesson about lasting riches. You might want to hang your poster in your room or on your locker door at school. A motto is a short sentence or phrase indicating a principle that is important to you.**

If time allows, have a few volunteers display their posters and explain why they chose the mottos they used.

Conclusion and Decision

CONCLUSION (3-5 minutes)

Have students turn to the section titled "Where Am I Investing?" in the Parchment. Ask them to work individually to follow the instructions in completing the section. Close in prayer and distribute the Fun Page as students leave.

Note: See the CONCLUSION activity of the next session for important pre-class preparation.

The Parchment

Obituary

Suppose you had to write the obituary notice for the rich fool. (An obituary is a public announcement of a person's death.) What would you have to say about him? Use your imagination a little and make sure to tell his possible strengths and weaknesses.

FOOL, THE RICH
Died April 1

Schwartz, Matthew

Matthew Schwartz, 48, longtime resident of our city, died early yesterday of a lingering illness. Mr. Schwartz was known by many for his gentle spirit and love for Jehovah. He leaves no relatives. Interment at 3:00 today from the Valley of Hinnom Mortuary. Mr. Schwartz's request, recorded by his friend and attendant Barney Johnson, is that in lieu of flowers, donations of full allegiance be made to Jesus of Nazareth.

Now write an obituary column for yourself. How would your life be viewed by others and by God if you died today?

—— Obituary ——

Where Am I Investing?

You've got a week's worth of potential. (Potential is what you *could* do with your life.) Let's call it $100.00 worth! Divide it up to show where your energy and effort went this week—and where you want it to go next week.

This Week	Next Week
God	God
Self	Self
Others in need	Others in need
Doing "nuthin'"	Doing "nuthin'"
My friends	My friends
Chores, job, sleeping, homework	Chores, job, sleeping, homework

FUN Page!

Session 9

"Command those who are rich in this present world not to be arrogant nor to put their hope in wealth, which is so uncertain, but to put their hope in God, who richly provides us with everything for our enjoyment. Command them to do good, to be rich in good deeds, and to be generous and willing to share. In this way they will lay up treasure for themselves as a firm foundation for the coming age, so that they may take hold of the life that is truly life."

1 Timothy 6:17-19

People die—that's the sad and tragic truth. It's especially tragic when the person who passed away spent his or her whole life being greedy and self-centered. But the Bible holds out the hope of eternal life for those who believe!

Sometimes it helps to understand a serious subject by examining it in the light of humor. With that in mind, let's take a look at this overcrowded graveyard's poetic

LAST WORDS:

DAILY NUGGETS
Wisdom from God's Word for you to read each day.

Day 1 Read Philippians 2:3,4. Whose interests should we look after? What attitude should we have toward others?

Day 2 Galatians 6:2-10. When we do good to others how are we sowing? What shall we reap?

Day 3 Proverbs 28:27. Think of a way you can regularly give of yourself or your possessions to others. Put it into practice this week.

Day 4 1 John 3:16-18. Is there a friend in need to whom you could show your love in a special way this week?

Day 5 James 2:15,16. Would the words of verse 16 be comforting to you if you were hungry

and cold? What action of love should be taken this week?

Day 6 2 Corinthians 5:15. Who should we live for?

HOT TOT

"Then he said to them, 'Watch out! Be on your guard against all kinds of greed; a man's life does not consist in the abundance of his possessions.'"

Luke 12:15

THE COMPLETE JUNIOR HIGH BIBLE STUDY RESOURCE BOOK #3
© 1988 GL/LIGHT FORCE, VENTURA, CA 93006

THEME: True riches come from God.

Session 9

BIBLE STUDY OUTLINE

Introduce Revelation 3:13-22 by telling students that the passage focuses on what Jesus said to a church in Laodicea whose members had grown spiritually useless and inactive. Make the following points as time allows:

- VERSE 14: The word angel generally means messenger. In this verse, the word may refer to a heavenly messenger, a human minister at the church, or it may represent the spirit of the church. What is more important in this passage is the identity of the One who is speaking. Jesus says, "These are the words of the Amen, the faithful and true witness, the ruler of God's creation." In these words we see the authority of Christ—the authority of His faithfulness, His truthfulness and His power over creation.
- VERSES 15,16: Cold water is refreshing, and hot water can make one feel good—but lukewarm water is nauseating! The people at Laodicea had become spiritually nauseating to God. They weren't cold—they didn't supply spiritual refreshment. And they weren't hot—they didn't supply spiritual comfort. They had no real purpose or effect. They were just there.
- VERSE 17: This verse tells why the Laodiceans had grown so worthless. They had become wealthy. Because of their wealth, they felt no needs. Life was easy for them.
- When people have no felt needs or concerns, they tend to forget about God. That's a real danger in our day and age. We have so much compared to many people around the world, and so we are in danger of complacency. Why run to God if we have no troubles? Why look to Him for aid and comfort if we are comfortable? We must be careful to remain faithful to Him and dependent on Him—not on money.
- Jesus points out that their wealth and comfort was really an illusion. They were actually wretched, pitiful, poor, blind and naked. Yeech!
- VERSE 18: Jesus counsels the Laodiceans to become spiritually wealthy. Jesus mentions gold, white clothes and eye salve. History tells us that the city of Laodicea was famous for three

things: financial wealth, a well-developed textile industry and a popular eye salve. The three things that Jesus said they should come to Him for! The point of all this is simple: we must depend on God and nothing else. When we place our emphasis on possessions or other worldly things, we offend God and place our spiritual health in jeopardy.
- VERSES 18-22: For those Christians who listen to Christ, He offers restored fellowship and victory.

OBJECT LESSON: COLORED LENSES

Bring eyeglasses with pastel-tinted lenses (rose-colored is perfect). As you speak of people who depend on wealth rather than God, wear the glasses. With tongue in cheek, describe how wonderful the world looks through tinted lenses. Then point out that people who try to live without depending on the Lord are merely living an illusion.

DISCUSSION QUESTIONS

1. **Why do you feel Jesus emphasized His authority when He began His message to the Laodiceans?**

2. **Do you think that spiritual lukewarmness is a common problem for Christians? If so, what can be done about it?**

3. **Do you believe Christians who live under the threat of persecution in other countries find it easier to constantly stay close to the Lord? Explain.**

4. **Why do you suppose God wants us to depend on Him?**

THE COMPLETE
JUNIOR HIGH BIBLE STUDY
RESOURCE BOOK #3

THREE-WAY TUG-OF-WAR

Tie two or three ropes together to form the three-handled rope illustrated. Be sure the knot will not allow the ropes to slip.

Assemble three teams, one on each rope as in a standard tug-of-war game. Now mark three spots on the ground (with pieces of cloth or anything else handy) as shown below. The object is for teams to attempt to pull the knot in the rope over their spot on the ground. The team that does so wins.

BLINDFOLD BACON

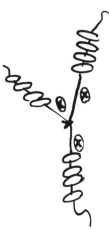

This is a steal-the-bacon game, but with blindfolds. Teams line up on opposite sides of a square. One member of each team is securely blindfolded. Toss a sock or other small object into the square. The object is for each of the blindfolded players to rush into the square (on hands and knees to avoid dangerous collisions), find the object and return it to his or her own team. Other team members shout directions to the blindfolded players. Allow all participants to have a turn at being blindfolded. The team with the most captures wins. If a team has one less player than the other, let a player on that team play twice. To make things more difficult and fun to watch, spin the blindfolded players until they are dizzy.

KNEES PLEASE

For any game where students must run, use masking tape to tape their knees together. Loads of laughs. And try taping ankles together for a three-way tug-of-war.

The Insensitive Spirit Session 10

INSIGHTS FOR THE LEADER

WHAT THE SESSION IS ABOUT

We have a responsibility to love others.

SCRIPTURE STUDIED

Luke 16:19-31

KEY PASSAGE

"The King will reply, 'I tell you the truth, whatever you did for one of the least of these brothers of mine, you did for me.'" Matthew 25:40

AIMS OF THE SESSION

During this session your learners will:

1. Tell what happened to the rich man and Lazarus;
2. Describe what might have happened if the rich man had shown compassion for Lazarus;
3. Show compassion by writing letters of inquiry to various relief agencies.

In this session you and your learners will be studying the parable of Lazarus and the rich man, as found in Luke 16:19-31. Jesus told this parable because of an interruption by the Pharisees. "The Pharisees, who loved money, heard all this and were sneering at Jesus" (Luke 16:14). Jesus had been teaching about the handling of wealth when they laughed at His teaching. He responded by telling this parable.

The message of the parable is twofold. First, Jesus dealt with the abuse of wealth, and secondly, He discussed the refusal of people to believe in the Resurrection.

The rich man in the parable is not named, but by tradition he has been called Dives (pronounced DIE-veez). Dives is the Latin word for rich. The poor man is named Lazarus. This is a transliteration of the Greek form of the Hebrew name Eleazar. The meaning of Eleazar is "God is my helper." Since names had special significance in biblical days, it may be that this man's name indicates that he was putting his trust in God to help him.

Jesus began by first telling of the rich man. He was dressed in purple, the most costly of dyes. He was clothed in linen, the most expensive cloth. He "lived in luxury every day" (v. 19). Luxury is an interesting word. In Greek the word is *lampros* which means "brilliantly." Thus, his manner of living was very flamboyant.

In contrast to this was the beggar, Lazarus. Lazarus, just outside the gate of the rich man, was in a pitiful condition. He was most probably lame, because the Scripture tells us he "was laid" at the gate (see v. 20). He was covered with open sores, which the wild dogs would come and lick. He was so weak that he could not even chase away these dogs, who were considered unclean by the Jews. All he wanted from the rich man was what fell from his table. He just wanted the rich man's garbage, and he had to fight the dogs for that!

The Hereafter

Thus, one man was very rich and the other was very poor. But there is more to life than the here and now. There is the hereafter. We are told that the poor man died, but we are not told that he was buried. Often the poor were taken to a place named the Valley of Hinnom, or Gehenna, where their bodies were burned. Yet Lazarus was carried by angels to Abraham's side, which was another way to say paradise to the Jewish listeners. Thus the crippled outcast had the privilege of close fellowship with God (implied in his being taken to Abraham's side).

"The rich man also died and was buried" (v. 22). But there were no angels for him, and no fellowship with God. His fate was different. He was in Hades, the place of torment. He was in agony.

Why did the poor man end up at Abraham's side? Surely not just because he was poor. And why did the rich man end up in Hades? Surely not just because he was rich. Rather, their fate was determined by their stance regarding God. As mentioned earlier, the name Lazarus means "God is my helper," and may indicate the trust this man put in the God of his people. On the other hand, the lack of compassion on the part of the rich man speaks loudly of his lack of concern for others, and is an indication of spiritual poverty.

In this world, the rich man had known no want; Lazarus had known plenty of want. After death, the roles were reversed. The rich man became the beggar, pleading for some relief from the flames. He addressed Abraham, the spiritual father of Israel. He cried for mercy. Lazarus, on the other hand, was no longer a beggar. He was comforted at the side of Abraham.

The rich man believed that Abraham would send Lazarus to him to serve him. He still thought of himself as superior to Lazarus. He thought that Lazarus was only his servant. He was not repentant, but was selfish yet. He could see only his desires. The fact that he knew the beggar's name reveals that he had known him before, but had never cared for him. With all his earthly wealth, he had not cared for the beggar near his gate.

Abraham told the rich man that his request was impossible to fulfill, because he and Lazarus were separated by a great chasm (see v. 26), and could not pass from one side to another. Then, still begging, the rich man asked for Lazarus to be sent back to communicate with his (the rich man's) brothers. He still saw Lazarus as a mere servant. He felt that if Lazarus returned from the dead, his brothers would turn from their selfishness.

Like other Jews of his time, the rich man was asking for a sign. Shortly after this parable the Jews were given a sign, when Jesus raised another Lazarus from the dead. (See John 11:1-44). But instead of believing as a result of the sign, they plotted to kill Jesus. (See John 11:45-57). Not even seeing the great miracle would turn them from their greed and selfishness. Perhaps Jesus was hinting at this future event when

He mentioned in the parable that the rich man's request was refused because it would not change the five brothers.

This parable is one of great sadness. The wealthy man had the means to help many. He could have used his money to tend to the needs of lots of hurting people. But he would not give. His selfish spirit stood in his way. His possession of this world's goods did not condemn him to hell, but his attitude toward those goods and toward God did.

Lessons to Be Learned

Jesus commanded us, "Give to the one who asks you, and do not turn away from the one who wants to borrow from you" (Matt. 5:42). He again warned us of judgment if we fail to minister to the needs of those around us. (See Matt. 25:34-39). And He said to those who did give to others in need, "I tell you the truth, whatever you did for one of the least of these brothers of mine, you did for me" (Matt. 25:40).

In the parable the rich man was insensitive to the needs of Lazarus. He was concerned only with himself and his own desires. In response to this story, your students need to examine their own lives and see if they have been like the rich man. Are they so busy enjoying themselves that they have neglected to look at others around them? Is there someone just outside their circle of friends who is lonely and hurting? Is someone begging for scraps of their attention? Have they demanded that their parents wait on them, rather than considering the needs of Mom and Dad?

Is there a lonely shut-in in the church to whom your students might write a letter, or a sick person they could visit? Do they know someone who needs help with cleaning, painting, yard work or child care? Might they consider collecting needed items for a missionary?

The rich man was so busy serving himself, he forgot to look beyond himself. Encourage your students to take to heart Jesus' warning of judgment and to begin serving others rather than just themselves.

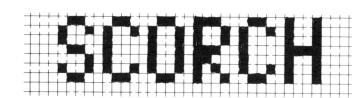
SESSION PLAN

BEFORE CLASS BEGINS: See the CONCLUSION for important information regarding relief organizations and their addresses. Photocopy the usual number of Parchment worksheets.

Attention Grabber

ATTENTION GRABBER (3-5 minutes)

As students arrive, give each one a copy of the Parchment student worksheet. Say, **Work the "What's the Message?" part of the Parchment.**

When most or all students have had a chance to find the solution, say something like, **As you can see, if you worked the puzzle correctly, the solution is SCORCH—a word which might help tip you off to today's subject. Our subject is the parable known as The Rich Man and Lazarus.**

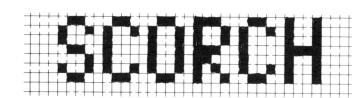

Bible Exploration

EXPLORATION (20-40 minutes)

Step 1 (8-10 minutes): On the left side of your chalkboard, in a column, write: *Housing; Food; Health; Clothes; Status; Contribution to Society.* To the right of the column, at the top of the board, write two headings: *Rich Man; Lazarus.* See sketch. Read, or ask one or more volunteers to read, Luke

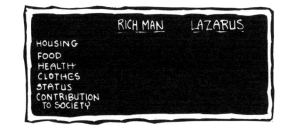

NOTES

16:19-31. Lead a discussion based on your chart, asking students to suggest what the rich man and Lazarus achieved in the areas listed in the column. Then briefly comment, **I imagine that most of us resemble the rich man more than Lazarus. Although you might think that you are really poor, when you compare some of our lowest standards of living with most of the people living in the world we look pretty rich. It is not wrong to be rich, but we must be careful not to make the same mistakes the rich man did.** Tell your students, **Let's read Luke 10:27 and discuss what the rich man in the parable could have done if he had loved Lazarus as he loved himself.**

Step 2 (8-10 minutes): Direct attention to the "Scorch-O-Gram" section of the Parchment student worksheet and tell students, **Work in groups of two or three to write a letter that the rich man might write from Hades to his brothers. Have him tell what he now realizes he did wrong, and what he wants his brothers to do differently so they can escape the judgment that has befallen him. It's not stated in so many words in the story, but you'll be able to figure it out by implication.** (Make sure students understand that the rich man did not go to Hades merely because he refused to help Lazarus. Rather, this refusal was a symptom of a whole style of life that left God out. The rich man didn't care about

Lazarus because he didn't care about God, and didn't know God personally. Helping the poor does not guarantee a person a place in heaven. It is not a way to earn salvation. But a salvation experience must be followed by evidence of Christlike behavior, which includes helping those in need.)

Step 3 (3-5 minutes): Regain students' attention and have a few volunteers read their letters. Again, make sure they understand the correct relationship of salvation and works.

OPTIONAL STEP 4 (10-15 minutes)

Tell students, **Write a parable of your own similar to the Lazarus parable. However, put it in a modern-day situation. For example, in place of Lazarus you could have a poor family with sick children. Put yourself in the parable in place of the rich man. Your ending may or may not turn out differently.** Allow students to work individually or in small groups. Circulate among them in order to encourage and to provide help if needed.

When students have finished, reassemble class and have a few volunteers read their parables. If time allows, discuss why people in the students' parables do what they do, and what the class can learn from their actions and the results of those actions.

Conclusion and Decision

CONCLUSION: (10-15 minutes)

Materials needed: Writing paper, envelopes, addresses of denominational and/or parachurch relief organizations (see the end of this session plan for several addresses.)

Explain, **We have seen how the rich man's** lack of a personal relationship with God was demonstrated by his lack of caring for the needs of Lazarus. Lazarus was right outside his gate, but the rich man chose to ignore him. Christians today have a responsibility to help those nearby, just as the rich man should have helped Lazarus. But, because we live in a time when we know more about the world around us, we also have a responsibility to help those who are further away. Also, if we live in a more affluent country, we have a special responsibility to see that some of our help goes to people in poorer countries. Therefore, today we're going to focus on channeling some help to people in poorer countries. One way to do this is through the relief agency of our own denomination or through relief agencies such as World Vision, Food for the Hungry, and others. Today we're going to write letters to find out what our class can do to help needy people in the world. When we get our answers we'll talk it over and decide what to do.

Provide paper and envelopes and the address(es) of the agency or agencies you have selected. Have students work individually to write letters inquiring how the class can help. Suggest, **Tell the organization what you've been studying and what conclusions you've come to, so they will understand what prompted your letter. Place your letters in your envelopes, but leave the envelopes unsealed.**

(After class, select two or three of the best letters addressed to each organization and send them as representative of your group.)

If you have time after students finish their letters, brainstorm things learners could do to help people in your local area, and develop a plan to actually carry out one of the ideas.

Close in prayer, asking God to sensitize your students and yourself to ways of meeting needs for others. Distribute the Fun Page.

ADDRESSES OF IMPORTANT RELIEF ORGANIZATIONS

Compassion International
3955 Cragwood Drive
P.O. Box 7000
Colorado Springs, CO 80933

(800) 336-7676

Compassion International is a nondenominational, evangelical organization helping more than 70,000 children in 31 countries.

Food for the Hungry
P.O. Box E
Scottsdale, AZ 85252

(602) 998-3100

Food for the Hungry helps provide for the physical and spiritual needs of millions of needy people. Offers both disaster relief and long-range self-help assistance.

Samaritan's Purse
Box 3000
Boone, NC 28607

(704) 262-1980

Working through missionaries and national churches to discover and meet the pressing needs of those often overlooked by others. The organization's president is Franklin Graham, Dr. Billy Graham's son.

World Vision International
919 W. Huntington Dr.
Monrovia, CA 91016

(818) 357-7979

A Christian relief and development organization helping the poor in the name of Christ in over 70 countries throughout the world.

Note: The next session, session 11, requires a few special materials including several pages of Sunday comics from the newspaper. See the EXPLORATION for details, page 127.

The Parchment

What's the Message?

There's a word hidden in the grid below. To decode the message, use a pencil or pen to fill in all the boxes (formed by the grid lines) that have three broken sides. Some boxes have no broken sides, some have one, some two, some three, and some four. Remember, shade only those boxes with three broken sides. An example has been done for you.

The word you find will give you a small hint about today's Bible story.

Scorch-O-Gram

Write a letter from the rich man to his brothers warning about the coming judgment and telling them how to treat others.

Dear Bros . . .

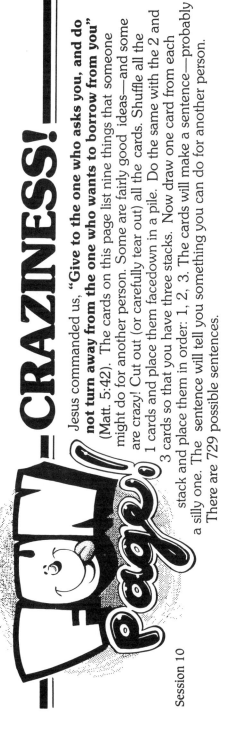

CRAZINESS!

Session 10

Jesus commanded us, **"Give to the one who asks you, and do not turn away from the one who wants to borrow from you"** (Matt. 5:42). The cards on this page list nine things that someone might do for another person. Some are fairly good ideas—and some are crazy! Cut out (or carefully tear out) all the cards. Shuffle all the 1 cards and place them facedown in a pile. Do the same with the 2 and 3 cards so that you have three stacks. Now draw one card from each stack and place them in order: 1, 2, 3. The cards will make a sentence—probably a silly one. The sentence will tell you something you can do for another person. There are 729 possible sentences.

1	2	3
I'd let you watch	your favorite TV show	to make you happy.
As the saying goes, "I worship	the ground you walk on,"	even though I don't know what that means.
I'd climb	the highest mountain	to be with you.
I'd drink from	the same cup you use	even if it made me sick.
I'd even baby-sit	your dumb brother	to make you happy.
I'd swim across	the deepest sea	even if I got soaked.
I'd let you borrow	my best coat	even if you failed to return it.
I'd let you wipe your nose on	my Kleenex	because that's the kind of person I am.
I'd stand in front of	a charging elephant	to save you.

DAILY NUGGETS Wisdom from God's Word for you to read each day.

Day 1 Read Hebrews 3:7-14. What can Christians do to guard against a hardened heart?

Day 2 Jonah 1:2. What had God asked Jonah to do? What was Jonah's response?

Day 3 Jonah 3:1-10. How did Jonah respond the second time God gave him instructions? How did Nineveh respond? What did God do?

Day 4 Jonah 4:1-11. Jonah was worried about his reputation if Nineveh escaped destruction. What, in verse 11, should Jonah have been more concerned about?

Day 5 Matthew 23:37-39. What attitude must a person have in order to receive God's blessings? How is your attitude?

Day 6 Luke 19:37-44. What did the disciples call Jesus? What name did the Pharisees use? What do their responses tell you about who they thought Jesus was?

HOT THOT

"The King will reply, 'I tell you the truth, whatever you did for one of the least of these brothers of mine, you did for me.'" **Matthew 25:40**

THEME: We have a responsibility to serve others.

Session 10

BIBLE STUDY OUTLINE

Begin your message with Ephesians 2:10: "For we are God's workmanship, created in Christ Jesus to do good works, which God prepared in advance for us to do." Now read Colossians 3:22-25 and make the following points as time allows:

- COLOSSIANS 3:22: As Ephesians 2:10 tells us, the Christian is created for good works. This passage in Colossians gives us insight into how we are to do good works. Paul, the author of Colossians, is speaking of literal slaves—but the principles of serving God by serving others still apply to us today. We are to obey with sincerity of heart and reverence for the Lord. Today, this means we should be quick to do as our parents, friends, teachers and bosses ask. Sometimes we don't like to do these things, but part of serving the Lord is to discipline ourselves to do things we don't like.
- VERSE 23: The best servants are those who want to do their finest for Jesus. Many Christians make the mistake of only looking to Jesus for things He can do for them—like some kind of cosmic Santa Claus. We must also ask ourselves what we should be doing *for* Him and because of Him.
- VERSE 24: Here's the good part! We are rewarded for our service. Some of the reward may be in this lifetime, some may be in heaven. But we will be rewarded for our service. We can't "out serve" God. He keeps track of every good thing we do and makes sure we are rewarded.
- VERSE 25: This verse speaks of the other side of the coin. People who do wrong will be punished, just as a bad slave was punished in Paul's day. Our God is not mean. When He punishes His child, His purpose is a good one. He desires that child to do right and earn reward. We are His children. We are to serve God by serving others. Make service a habit.

OBJECT LESSONS: VESSELS OF SERVICE

Bring a variety of vessels to show, such as a cup, a glass, a pot, a cake pan, a flower vase and a trash can. Also bring water in a container and a box or bag to carry everything in.

As you speak about being servants of God, show the vessels to everyone. Pour the water back and forth between vessels, demonstrating the capacity of each.

Say, **God wants to use us, and we are to serve Him. Like these vessels, each of us has a different function and purpose for which we were designed. And like the water that fills these vessels, God wants to fill us—with Himself through the Holy Spirit. Then He will use us to pour out His love in service to others. God created us to serve Him. Are we allowing Him to use us?**

DISCUSSION QUESTIONS

1. **What are some good works Christians can and should be doing?**

2. **What does "sincerity of heart" and "reverence for the Lord"—as mentioned in Col. 3:22—mean? What do they have to do with serving God?**

3. **Why must we sometimes do things we don't like to do? What would happen if we all suddenly decided we weren't going to do things we don't wish to do?**

4. **Why does God sometimes discipline His children? What are some ways He might discipline?**

5. **How can we make good works a habit?**

THE COMPLETE
JUNIOR HIGH BIBLE STUDY
RESOURCE BOOK #3

A mixed bag of fun.

COKE MACHINE

When it's time to pass out refreshments, designate one person with pants pockets to be the "Coke machine." He or she places a soft drink bottle or can in a back pocket, opens it and pours the contents into the cup of the first person in line. The catch is, the cola must stay in the pocket and not be touched by hands while pouring. This stunt is a real mess, so do it outside or on a plastic drop cloth.

COOKIE ART

Organize a cookie baking party. Participants use ready-made cookie batter to create outrageous faces or other silly designs. After the cookies come out of the oven, the cookies are decorated with various confections. Have a "judge-off" and award prizes for several categories.

To motivate players who may think cookie baking is beneath their dignity, make the cookies for a worthy cause such as the next Sunday's little children's class.

WATERLESS MARCO POLO

Marco Polo and Silent Marco Polo are two popular swimming pool games. You can play them in a room by allowing participants to play on their knees. Here's how: Have all participants get down on hands and knees. Blindfold one player. When that player calls out "Marco," all other players must respond "Polo." When the blindfolded player hears the response, he or she scurries toward the sound, hoping to tag one of the other players. A player who is tagged then must wear the blindfold. The players always try to avoid being tagged, of course, but they may never stand to run away. They must also stay within any boundary line you've set. They must always respond when the blindfolded player yells, "Marco." (Silent Marco Polo is played without the sound effects. In this case, blindfolded players must listen very carefully for the sound of the other players' rustling or giggling.)

The Rebellious Spirit Session 11

INSIGHTS FOR THE LEADER

WHAT THE SESSION IS ABOUT

People rebel against God's rule.

SCRIPTURE STUDIED

Luke 20:9-16.

KEY PASSAGE

"For you were like sheep going astray, but now you have returned to the Shepherd and Overseer of your souls." 1 Peter 2:25

AIMS OF THE SESSION

During this session your learners will:

1. Retell the parable of the vineyard and the tenants;
2. Discuss implications of this parable in their lives;
3. Consider acknowledging their rebellion and asking for forgiveness.

In this session you and your students will examine the parable of the rebellious tenants as found in Luke 20:9-16. The parable may be summarized in the words of John: "He came to that which was his own, but his own did not receive him" (John 1:11).

Christ's Authority

In this section of Scripture we see Jesus as a man of strength and authority. He was not Jesus the meek and mild, but Jesus the King. He had just entered Jerusalem on a donkey (see Luke 19:28-44). This was a clear declaration that He was king and that He was coming in peace. He was fulfilling Zechariah 9:9. He chose a donkey colt because the donkey was considered a noble beast and was used by kings when they rode with peaceful intent. Only on the battlefield did kings ride horses.

Having entered Jerusalem in a manner indicating His claim to be King of the Jews, Jesus next stormed the Temple without an army (see Luke 19:45,46). Here was the boldness of our Lord. He declared, after single-handedly chasing the merchants out, "It is written, . . . 'My house will be a house of prayer'; but you have made it 'a den of robbers'" (Luke 19:46). Not only was Jesus claiming to be King of the Jews, He was implying His deity by exerting His right to clean up the corruption in the Temple. No wonder the religious establishment demanded to know the source of His authority (see Luke 20:1,2). Instead of answering the question directly, Jesus used the parable of the tenants to speak to them of their rebellion and of His own coming death.

The Parable of the Tenants

The parable tells about a man who planted a vineyard and then rented it to some farmers while he went away. When harvest time came, the owner sent a servant to collect the payment due from the tenants. But the tenants beat up the servant and refused to pay the rent. The owner sent a second servant, and then a third, but they received the same treatment. Finally the owner sent his own son, thinking the tenants would respect him. Instead, they killed the son, hoping to gain the vineyard for themselves. According to Jesus, the owner of the vineyard "will come and kill those tenants and give the vineyard to others" (Luke 20:16).

The picture Jesus drew in the parable is from Isaiah 5:1-7, where Israel is described as God's vineyard. Thus, the vineyard in the parable is the nation of Israel. The owner of the vineyard is God. The farmers are the priests and rulers of Israel. The mistreated servants are the prophets. And the murdered son is Jesus Christ Himself.

We might wonder how the farmers could get away with stealing this piece of property. Palestine had a number of situations similar to

this one. Someone would plant a vineyard, build a wall and rent the field to a tenant farmer. The farmer could pay the owner in any one of three agreed-upon ways. He might pay a certain amount per year for use of the field. He might pay a certain percentage of the crop grown. Or he might pay a certain quantity of the crop, regardless of the crop size. All of this was contracted before the renter took possession of the vineyard. Because the times were so troubled and travel so unsafe, sometimes a man would not live to see his property again. The land would fall into the possession of the tenant farmer if no kin of the owner could be found.

Matthew's Gospel indicates that this vineyard had been treated in the most careful way. It had a hedge around it to keep out animals, a watch tower to protect it from robbers and a winepress to produce wine (see Matt. 21:33). Everything had been done to ensure that it would produce the choicest of wine. This same care had been given to Israel. God always takes care of His own. He is tireless in His care for those who love Him.

Yet all the vineyard owner's care was met with rebellion. He was not making severe demands. All he wanted was that which was owed to him. He was patient. He sent three servants to collect what was owed, but all were beaten. (See Luke 20:10-12). Without anger or wrath, he finally sent his son. Yet the son was treated worse than the servants. His blood was upon the hands of the farmers. What was the only just thing for the owner to do? "He will come and kill those tenants and give the vineyard to others" (v. 16).

God's final response is judgment and death for those who refuse to respond to His servants and His Son.

Today's Tenants

Even today we find ourselves in the position of tenants, guarding and working with the resources that God has given us. The danger comes when we assume that what we tend is what we own.

The bottom line of almost all spiritual rebellion (in adults or in teenagers) is a matter of ownership. God holds our very existence on His fingertip. But we foolishly (even as Christians) claim our rights to govern areas of our own lives for our own pleasure.

Rent is due but the tenants have claimed the ground as their own, with disastrous results.

Those little seeds of rebellion seem to sprout quickly in junior high years. The natural desire for independence from parental control can lead to a rebellion against all control or authority—including God's.

Some of your students in their struggle to think for themselves may have decided to claim for themselves something that is not really theirs—their lives.

God tells us that we have been bought with a price, the blood of Christ (see 1 Cor. 6:20). The question of ownership is settled but the rebellion of the foolish tenants goes on. Jesus told this parable in the hope that we would not be caught up in that rebellion ourselves.

NOTES

SESSION PLAN

BEFORE CLASS BEGINS: See the EXPLORATION for special materials required; photocopy the Parchment student worksheet.

Attention Grabber

ATTENTION GRABBER (1-2 minutes)

When students have been seated, say, **'Don't boss me around!' Where would you be most likely to hear these words?** Ask for a few volunteers to respond.

Make a transition to the EXPLORATION by saying, **You've mentioned several situations in which people don't want to be bossed. In fact, most people don't like to be bossed around at all. God doesn't want to boss us, but He does expect us to give Him the honor and respect He deserves. Since He knows what is best and loves us enough to want the best for us, He wants us to obey Him because we want to, not because anyone forces us to. Today we will look at a story that Christ told that illustrates this principle.**

Bible Exploration

EXPLORATION (25-35 minutes)

Materials needed: Sheets of newsprint or butcher paper, felt pens in various colors, several comic page sections from the Sunday paper, scissors and glue.

Step 1 (12-15 minutes): Present a brief introduction giving the background of the parable of the vineyard and the tenants, using material from the INSIGHTS FOR THE TEACHER. Then have students form groups of three to four. Read Luke 20:9-16 aloud while the students follow in their own Bibles.

Distribute paper, felt pens, scissors, comics and glue. Explain, **I want each group to make a cartoon version of the story we have just read. Instead of drawing the figures, use the scissors to cut out cartoons from the comic pages I have given you. Glue the cartoons to**

127

Your students may wish to see this solution to the Fun Page Puzzle.

(If you like, write the solution on an extra copy of the Fun Page and pin it to your classroom bulletin board.)

your newsprint. **Use the pens to add dialogue and anything else you need to complete your comic strips. You can update this parable as if it happened today.** It is not necessary to reveal the meaning of Christ's parable; students will have the opportunity to understand His meaning in a few minutes.

Step 2 (3-5 minutes): Reassemble the class and let each group display and read its comic strip. As each is read, correct any mistaken ideas and add any important concepts that the groups may have missed.

Step 3 (10-12 minutes): Discuss who the following characters represent: The landlord (represents God); the servants (the prophets God had sent in former times who were rejected—usually violently); the son (God's Son, Jesus Christ); the tenants (the Jews). Ask your listeners who they think the tenants would be today. Supplement students' ideas as needed with information from INSIGHTS FOR THE TEACHER.

Also discuss the following questions (see INSIGHTS FOR THE TEACHER for information

needed): **Where did the tenants go wrong?** (They tried to keep what was not theirs.) **Why do you think they rebelled?** (Opinion question.) **What should they have done? Why?** (They should have paid their rent; it was agreed upon in advance and it was the owner's right to receive it.) **What do you think God wants from us?** (He wants what is due Him—our praise and respect and obedience.) **Why do people not give God what He wants?** (The nature of sinful humankind is to do what we want rather than what God wants.) **What is the outcome if one continually refuses to give God His due?** (Such a person, never having received God's gift of eternal life, is condemned to spend eternity apart from God and all the good things He has made.) **What can happen to Christians if they rebel against God in specific areas?** (God will discipline them in order to bring them back to Himself. See Heb. 12:5-11.)

Conclusion and Decision

CONCLUSION (2-3 minutes)

Have students turn to "What Kind of Tenant Am I?" section of student worksheet and tell them, **We are all just tenants on this earth. Sooner or later we'll be called on to be accountable for our stay here. This session gives us an opportunity to think about what kind of tenants we are being. Use the Parchment to help you think it through.**

Allow time for students to complete the assignment. Then close in prayer. Distribute the Fun Page.

ALTERNATE CONCLUSION (3-5 minutes)

Have students turn to "Where's the Rebellion?" section of the Parchment student worksheet. Tell them, **Work alone to answer the questions about your own areas of rebellion. Then, if you are ready to ask for God's forgiveness and help for your rebellion, fill in the bottom part.**

Close in prayer and hand out the Fun Page.

WHERE'S THE REBELLION?

I tend to rebel against doing what God wants me to do in the following area(s):

- ☐ Obeying my parents
- ☐ Loving my enemies
- ☐ Self-control
- ☐ Choice of friends
- ☐ Use of time
- ☐ Use of money

- ☐ In my speech
- ☐ In self-discipline
- ☐ Honesty
- ☐ Reading God's Word
- ☐ Being kind to people
- ☐ Forgiving others

- ☐ Showing patience
- ☐ Having prejudice
- ☐ Being responsible
- ☐ Being grateful

God, please forgive me for my rebellious attitude toward you in:

Help me to:

WHAT KIND OF TENANT AM I?

Believe it or not, you are just a tenant on this earth. Sooner or later you'll be called on to be accountable for your stay here. Wouldn't it be much better to meet your heavenly landlord with your rent paid up? In order to do that you need to figure out what kind of tenant you are. Choose one of the following.

I tend to be . . .

- ○ A rebellious tenant.
- ○ A careless tenant.
- ○ Spending my rent on other interests.
- ○ A good tenant.

I want to be . . .

THE VINEYARD!

Session 11

In Jesus' parable of the tenant farmers (see Luke 20:9-16), some evil people tried to take over a man's vineyard by beating his servants and killing his son. Jesus was talking about the way people persecuted the prophets of old and eventually crucified Jesus, God's Son. Things were not right in the vineyard, that's for sure. In fact, they—well, to find out what we mean, work this simple puzzle. Here's how: There are hundreds of grapes in the illustration. Some of the grapes contain a tiny dot. With a pen or pencil, fill in the grapes with the dot to spell out the solution to our puzzle.

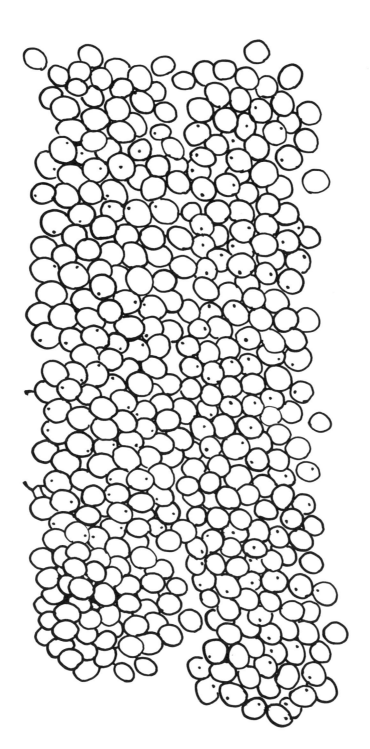

DAILY NUGGETS Wisdom from God's Word for you to read each day.

Day 1 Read Romans 5:17-21. What is the end result of transgression or sin? Through whom is eternal life provided?

Day 2 Hebrews 12:14-17. What must Christians make every effort to be? What happens without this quality? What is the lesson we can learn from Esau's mistake?

Day 3 Isaiah 1:18-20. Put this passage into your own words so it speaks to people such as your friends.

Day 4 Colossians 3:2-17. What are the characteristics of someone who is resisting Christ? What are the qualities a Christian should have?

Day 5 Matthew 12:33-37. Why are words so

important? Have your words been uplifting lately?

Day 6 Ephesians 4:11-24. How are Christians not to walk (live)? If you have received what Jesus taught, what happens to you (verses 22-24)?

"For you were like sheep going astray, but now you have returned to the Shepherd and Overseer of your souls."

1 Peter 2:25

THEME: Put on the new self.

Session 11

BIBLE STUDY OUTLINE

Read Ephesians 4:17-24 to your listeners. Make these points as time allows (being sensitive to the fact that there may be non-Christians in your class):

- VERSES 17-19: Paul insists that we Christians are no longer to behave like non-Christians do. They have dim understanding of God and are separated from Him because they have "hardening of their hearts" (verse 18). Their hearts have become calloused and insensitive, and they are continually searching to indulge themselves in the things of this world, which Paul calls "every kind of impurity" (see verse 19). An impurity in a diamond wrecks the value of that diamond—and the impurity of sin in a human being wrecks the relationship between that person and God.
- VERSES 20-23: Christians, on the other hand, are to behave in a brand new way. We are to "put off" our former way of life, our old non-Christian selves, and be made new in our attitudes. Our new attitudes will influence the way we think, the way we feel and the things we do. A Christian with this new attitude is a changed human being, a new creation with a completely different style of living. And so we see in this passage a stark contrast between non-Christians and Christians. As Christians, we must be different from the rest. We must change. We can't go on doing the same old sinful things that we used to do. This is one reason it's not always easy to be a Christian. But with God's power, we can be the people He wants us to be.
- VERSE 24: We were told to put off the old self, now we are told to put on the new self. [At this point, do the OBJECT LESSON.]

OBJECT LESSON: DIRTY SOCKS

Wear white socks under your shoes, socks that have been thoroughly soiled. Bring a clean pair of socks to change into.

As you speak, remove your shoes and dirty socks. Show your listeners the dirty socks and say something like, **These socks represent the old life. To another pair of dirty socks, these are perfectly fine, wonderful socks. But to you and me, they're gross. In the same way, a non-Christian might seem perfectly fine and wonderful to some, but to God there's a great problem. He wants each of us to put on a new attitude, a new behavior and a new style of life.** Put on the clean socks and shoes. Say, **There, that's much better.**

Wrap up the body of your message by pointing out that the Ephesians passage has drawn a contrast between the dark world of the non-Christian and the light-filled world of the believer. Encourage students to walk in a manner worthy of the Lord. Be available after class to explain God's plan of salvation to any student who expresses an interest.

DISCUSSION QUESTIONS

1. **What does it mean to be "separated from the life of God" (see verse 18)?**

2. **Define the words *sensitivity, sensuality, impurity* and *lust*.**

3. **Name some of the behavior and attitudes Christians need to avoid.**

4. **In what way does removing the dirty socks relate to the relationship between God and an unbeliever?**

5. **A sock can be washed clean. How can a non-Christian become clean? How can a Christian who sins become clean?**

GL LIGHT FORCE

THE COMPLETE
JUNIOR HIGH BIBLE STUDY
RESOURCE BOOK #3

A couple of silly games and some music to soothe the soul.

PIANO RELAY

If you have a piano in your play room, try this crazy relay race. Form two teams. Gather both teams around the piano and show them how to play with one finger a silly song of seven or eight notes. (Choose an easily recognized lead-in to a popular song or use that ditty with no name that people try to knock on doors with, which is played with these notes: F C C D C E F.

Now form your teams in two rows near the wall opposite the piano. At a signal to start, the first player in each row runs to the piano and plays the first note of the song (one player on a low octave, the other player on a high octave). The players then run back to their respective teams and tag the next players in line. Those players run to the piano and play the first and second notes of the song. The third players must play the first, second and third notes. This continues until one player correctly plays the entire song. His or her team wins. If a wrong note is struck by someone, that player must tag the next player in line who must then correctly play the proper notes.

In the heat of battle, so many mistakes will be made that probably everyone on each team will have at least one chance to play the piano. In fact, you may have to call a halt before the song is correctly done!

CRAB RELAY

This is a standard relay race (or any variation you like to play) with one small change. Players must run "crab style" as illustrated.

EDUCATIONAL PITCH PENNY

Most kids know how to play pitch penny, which is a gambling game and therefore not widely accepted in church! However, you can take the gambling out of it and turn it into an educational game. Here's how: Participants play the standard way by standing on a mark several feet from a wall and pitching a coin or similar object at the base of the wall. Instead of trying to win the game by landing the coin closer to the wall than anyone else, players try to hit targets which you've drawn on a large sheet of paper. Your targets can contain Scripture references of your own choosing. The player who hits a target reads the passage aloud. Players score points for each hit.

You could also create "Question" and "Answer" targets. One player hits a target containing an important question, another player aims for the target containing the appropriate answer. The two players work as partners to defeat other couples.

The Trustworthy Spirit Session 12

INSIGHTS FOR THE LEADER

WHAT THE SESSION IS ABOUT

What God has given us, we must use for His glory.

SCRIPTURE STUDIED

Matthew 25:14-30

KEY PASSAGE

"His master replied, 'Well done, good and faithful servant! You have been faithful with a few things; I will put you in charge of many things. Come and share your master's happiness!'" Matthew 25:21

AIMS OF THE SESSION

During this session your learners will:

1. Chart the events in the lives of the servants in the parable of the talents;
2. Determine what talents God has given them to use;
3. Offer these abilities to God in prayer; plan at least one way to use an ability in God's service.

In this session you and your students will examine the parable of the talents as found in Matthew 25:14-30. The parable is concerned with taking the resources that God has given us and using them to glorify Him. The expression "Use it or lose it!" is a good summary of the parable. The central theme of this story is using the gifts God gives to us to show our faithfulness to Him. The desire of every Christian is for the Lord to say, "Well done, good and faithful servant!" (v. 21).

Immediately before telling this parable, Jesus had spoken of the end of the age and His return (see Matt. 24). He stressed what His followers should be doing while awaiting His coming. He told the parable of the ten virgins, stressing the need for watchfulness. Now, in this parable of the talents, Jesus stressed the need for faithfulness in using our resources for Him.

The parable involves a wealthy man who was going away for a long trip. During his absence he was entrusting his property to his servants (literally, his slaves). This property consisted of a large sum of money. One servant was given five talents, another two talents, and the third, one talent.

A talent was a weight equivalent to about 75 pounds. At the time, the standard metal coin was silver, so a talent was 75 pounds of silver. As indicated in Session 8, a talent was equal to 6,000 days' wages for a common laborer, or 16½ years of work. (Students might also be interested in the current market value of 75 pounds of silver if you are able to get the per-ounce price.)

The servant entrusted with five talents had about 82 years' worth of money; the servant with two talents, 33 years' worth; and the servant with one talent had 16 ½ years' worth. Each man was given a responsibility in accordance with his ability. The master was not going to take a chance of losing this amount of money, so he selected his servants carefully, choosing those he thought he could trust.

Use of Talents

The man given five talents went immediately to work. He felt he had been honored with the trust of his master. Likewise, the servant with two talents went to work right away. These two servants took seriously the demands of their master. Having been honored by the master, they wanted to honor him.

The third servant's reaction was different. He took the valuable silver, dug a hole and buried it. He took the lazy way out. He would relax, take it easy and give back just what had been given to him.

After a long period of time, the master returned. The day of reckoning had come. The first servant had doubled his five talents, and with joy over his faithful stewardship, he brought the sum to his master. He received the

NOTES

praise of his master: "Well done, good and faithful servant!" (Matt. 25:21). He also received a promise of greater responsibility in the future.

Likewise, the second servant came with his talents. He, too, had doubled his master's property. He, too, was complimented on his faithfulness and promised more responsibility in the future.

At last the third servant approached, having dug up the talent entrusted to him. He began by making excuses. He said that he failed to invest the money for fear of losing it.

The master's reply to his servant was, "You wicked, lazy servant!" (Matt. 25:26). He told the servant that he should have put the money in the bank and at least collected interest. The master recovered the money and gave it to the servant who had ten talents.

What was Jesus telling us through this parable? He was speaking of the use of resources. The two good servants made a proper use of resources and were rewarded accordingly; the bad servant refused to use his resources at all, and was punished accordingly.

Another application of the parable is seen in the way the word talent has come to mean a gift or ability. We can look at the parable as a warning to use for our Master the gifts, abilities and other resources He has given us.

SESSION PLAN

BEFORE CLASS BEGINS: Photocopy the Parchment and Fun Page.

Attention Grabber

ATTENTION GRABBER (3-5 minutes)

When class is ready to begin, say, **Pretend that someone you know has just given you a thousand dollars. You are not to spend the money on yourself. Instead, you are to wisely invest the money so that when your friend returns in a year, you can give him or her even more money. What are some ways you'd invest the money?**

Allow a few volunteers to respond. Make a transition to the next part of the session by saying, **Our story today is about a man who went away and trusted his money to several servants. We'll see how the servants responded to this opportunity to prove their trustworthiness.**

Bible Exploration

NOTES

EXPLORATION (30-40 minutes)

Step 1 (10-12 minutes): Read Matthew 25:14-30 aloud while students follow in their own Bibles. Then lead a discussion based on the section of the Parchment titled, "The Talented Servants." Have students fill in the blanks on their worksheets as the discussion proceeds.

Step 2 (8-10 minutes): Assemble students into groups of three to five. Explain, **Write a want ad you think the master might have written in order to get a servant to replace the one he dismissed.** Each group should write its ad on a blank sheet of paper or on the back of the Parchment.

Step 3 (5-7 minutes): Have groups share their efforts with the rest of the class.

Step 4 (8-10 minutes): Explain that the parable means that God wants His people to take the gifts and abilities and talents that He gives them and use these for His glory. Lead a discussion using questions like these: **What talents or abilities does God entrust us with today?** (Personality traits, possessions, skills, knowledge and so on.) **What are we to do with our gifts, talents and abilities?** (Use them in a way that lets other people see God's work, God's love and God's creativity in us.) **What could we do with them instead?** (We could waste them, refuse to use them at all or use

them for unworthy purposes.) **What do you think happens when our abilities are used for God?** (He is pleased, other people are helped and we ourselves benefit by receiving more opportunities for service.) **What could we be doing to use the gifts or potential that God has given us for His benefit?** (Helping others, growing in Christ, etc. Draw specific, concrete ideas from your students that relate to your particular church and community situation as well as to broader world needs.) **What would be some results of not using our abilities for God?** (God is disappointed and we lose the benefits that we would otherwise gain; other people miss out on the help we could have provided to them.) **What would be different in these situations if we did use our abilities for God?** (God would be pleased and therefore we would sense His approval and would feel good about Him and about ourselves; other people would be helped; we ourselves would gain the benefits of added responsibility and opportunities to serve.)

Make a transition to the next part of the session by saying, **We've had a chance to look at Jesus' teaching about using our talents for Him. We'll conclude by thinking about the personal application of what we have learned.**

Conclusion and Decision

CONCLUSION (7-9 minutes)

Tell students, **Find one other person that you would like to get together with for this activity. Then write down one area in which your partner has some talent or potential that could be used for God. If you're uncertain, ask questions such as "What are you good at doing? What do you like to do? What skills or actions are easy for you?" Then exchange papers.** After students have exchanged papers say, **Now write on the paper at least one way you plan to use your talent or ability in God's service.**

After allowing time for students to complete the assignment, close in a brief audible prayer, offering the students' abilities to God.

Distribute the Fun Page.

Note: The final session, session 13, requires a bit of pre-class preparation if you wish to do the OPTIONAL part of the ATTENTION GRABBER. See page 147 for details.

The Parchment

The Talented Servants
Based on Matthew 25:14-30

	Servant #1	Servant #2	Servant #3
What did the master entrust him with?			
How did the master decide how much to give him?			
What did the servant do with it?			
How much profit was made?			
How much did he return to the master?			
What did the master call him?			
What reason did the master give?			
What words would you use to describe the relationship between the master and the servant?			
What qualities do you think you see in this servant?			

> **A talent was worth about 16 years of work for a common laborer.**

TANGLED TALENTS!

The Bible indicates that God is happy when we use our talents and abilities faithfully (see the HOT THOT below). We made a short list of different talents and things that you could use in God's service, but we messed up: the list has been scrambled in an unusual way. Each word broke into two parts, and the parts were reassembled in the wrong order. Your job is to split each word into two parts and then arrange the parts to make the correct words. The only trouble is, you don't know where to split the scrambled words, and you don't know what the correct words are! Good luck. The answers are upside down below.

MUSITATION
DRANESSING
MOPING
VICHING
CARSIC
WITNEY
TEAWING
HELDNESS
KINING

DAILY NUGGETS

Day 1 Read Titus 1:7-9. What will the good overseer be able to do (verse 9)?

Day 2 1 Corinthians 4:1,2. Do you consider yourself a servant of Christ? What is required of a servant?

Day 3 1 Peter 4:8-10. What three things are Christians asked to do? Which of these is above all? Why?

Day 4 1 Thessalonians 2:4. If you are a Christian, is there someone with whom you can share what Jesus has done for you?

Day 5 Luke 19:12-17. What does the Lord want us to do with the gifts He gives us? How can you use your gifts to reap benefits for the Lord this week?

Day 6 Luke 12:35-42. What are we to be when the Lord returns? Do you have a servant's heart?

ANSWERS: Music (you could lead songs or play guitar for your youth group), **drawing** (for the youth group newsletter), **money** (contributing to godly ministries), **visitation** (seeing someone in the hospital), **kindness**, **witnessing** (telling another about Jesus), **caring**, **helping** (you could set up chairs at a meeting), **teaching** (leading a simple Bible study).

"His master replied, 'Well done, good and faithful servant! You have been faithful with a few things; I will put you in charge of many things. Come and share your master's happiness!'"

Matthew 25:21

THEME: The qualifications of one who would serve God.

Session 12

BIBLE STUDY OUTLINE

Tell your listeners that you are going to take a look at the qualifications of an overseer (called "bishop" in some versions) listed in Titus 1:7-9. Make these points as time allows:

- VERSE 7: In this passage, an overseer is a person who holds a special responsibility of caring for other Christians. You aren't overseers right now, but the qualifications we see in this passage are qualifications that are good for any Christian to have, so I want to take a look at them with you. First of all, Paul, the author of Titus, says that an overseer is a person who has been entrusted with God's work. You may not realize it yet, but God does have a job and purpose which He has entrusted to you. Ephesians 2:10 says, "For we are God's workmanship, created in Christ Jesus to do good works, which God prepared in advance for us to do." So God has some important assignment for you, and part of the adventure of your Christianity is to find out what He has in mind for you.

- Paul now gives a list of qualifications of the overseer. He must be blameless—not overbearing (which means he should be a leader but not a slave driver), not quick-tempered, not a drunkard, not violent, and not pursuing dishonest gain.

- VERSE 8: Now Paul lists some "do's." An overseer must be hospitable (kind, generous, sensitive to the needs of others), one who loves good (a seemingly rare commodity in this world), self-controlled, upright, holy and disciplined. Of all these qualifications, *discipline* is perhaps the rarest of all among people your age. Not military-style discipline, but simply the quality of sticking to God and godliness when the going gets rough. So many young Christians "bomb out" on God just because they want to follow their friends or because it's hard to take a stand for Jesus. Discipline is rare and that's why it is so important that you examine your own self and seek to develop a greater personal discipline.

- VERSE 9: Finally, Paul points out that the overseer must hold firmly to the teachings of the Bible. So must we all. The Word of

God is the truth, and truth is our foundation on which we build our lives. Without that firm foundation, a person cannot last. A Christian who strays from God's truth will end up with a ton of troubles.

- Examine yourselves. Do you meet these qualifications? If so, congratulations! If not, do something about it. You are welcome to talk with me later, if you wish.

SHORT STORY: QUALIFICATIONS

Describe to your students the qualifications that were required for you to get your job. You might also discuss with students the qualifications required for other professions such as mechanic, doctor, pilot, secretary or gardener. Talk about the preparation it took to develop your qualifications (the time, concentration, and personal discipline). Relate the idea of job qualifications to a Christian's personal qualifications (the importance, time, concentration and discipline required).

DISCUSSION QUESTIONS

1. **What are some of the jobs God may entrust to Christians your age?**

2. **How can a person find out what job God has in mind?**

3. **Why is personal discipline so important to the Christian's life? What is personal discipline, anyway? How can we develop it?**

THE COMPLETE
JUNIOR HIGH BIBLE STUDY
RESOURCE BOOK #3

Some fun with slide projectors.

MEGA MAZE

Buy a book of mazes (you can find some great ones in the games section of the large chain bookstores). Take slides of several of the mazes and project them one at a time against a paper drop cloth taped to the wall. Give everyone markers and let them try to be the first to solve each maze. Mass confusion!

SLIDE ART

Buy or make clear slides (glue plastic squares—the kind of plastic used for photocopy machines, since other plastics might melt—into slide frames). Make enough slides for each pair of students to have one (with a few extra for use if necessary). Pairs work together with felt markers to create tiny drawings which can be projected. Each slide is part of a longer story that the whole group is working on. The story can be from the Bible, or a special presentation such as a silly way to announce an upcoming event. Naturally, the art won't be great—but it's fun.

SILLY SILHOUETTES

Hang a large bed sheet in such a way that it can be lit from the back by the projector beam. The audience tries to guess the identities of several kids who reveal their silhouettes from behind the sheet. Guessing can be made harder by standing the people making the silhouettes a little away from the sheet so that their shadows are out of focus.

This is also fun for skits. Participants perform a skit behind the sheet. A good example is a farcical surgery performed on a hapless patient by several nutty doctors. The doctors can pretend (and appear in silhouette) to saw the patient in half with a hand saw. Props, such as plastic body parts, can be tossed out from behind the sheet. Yeech!

The Persistent Spirit

WHAT THE SESSION IS ABOUT

Christians should persist in prayer and loyalty to God.

SCRIPTURE STUDIED

Matthew 6:7,8; 24:12,13; Luke 18:1-8.

KEY PASSAGE

"And will not God bring about justice for his chosen ones, who cry out to him day and night? Will he keep putting them off?" Luke 18:7

AIMS OF THE SESSION

During this session your students will:
1. Study the parable of the persistent widow;
2. Discuss persistent prayer and loyalty to God;
3. Pledge themselves to seek God persistently.

INSIGHTS FOR THE LEADER

This session focuses on the parable of the persistent widow, found in Luke 18:1-8. Jesus told this story to His disciples "to show them that they should always pray and not give up" (v. 1). He also made a second application by asking, "When the Son of Man comes, will he find faith on the earth?" (v. 8), a reference to the spiritual state of affairs just before Christ's return.

The Unrighteous Judge

Jesus begins His story by describing a judge "who neither feared God nor cared about men" (v. 2). The judge was unconcerned about the needs and opinions of people. Because he had no respect for God, he had no motivation to care about justice. A person with no respect for God may see little reason to respect others. Conversely, a Christian who knows the Lord as a just God must be concerned about justice for all. Historically, Christians have fought for prison reform, establishment of child labor laws, and political freedom. A young Christian can demonstrate a sense of righteous justice by showing kindness to an unpopular student, for example.

The Persistent Widow

In Jesus' day, perhaps even more than today, a widow was at a severe disadvantage. Without family, a woman's economic situation was desperate. All the more important, then, was the ability to obtain justice from the judicial system in time of need.

The widow in the parable had a problem, not detailed by Christ. Whatever the cause, she kept coming to the judge "with the plea, 'Grant me justice against my adversary'" (v. 3). The judge refused her for some time, but finally gave in because of her persistence. As he put it, "Even though I don't fear God or care about men, yet because this widow keeps bothering me, I will see that she gets justice, so that she won't eventually wear me out with her coming!" (vv. 4,5).

The Meaning

In verses 6-8, Jesus makes plain the meaning of His story. He contrasts the nature of the unjust judge, who had to be coerced into answering the widow's pleas, to God who "will see that they get justice, and quickly." In other words, our God happily answers prayers.

An important point of the parable is the idea of persistence. A young reader may misinterpret the parable to mean that Christians are supposed to hound God until He responds. Actually, persistence in prayer has nothing to do with "babbling like pagans, for they think they will be heard because of their many words" (Matthew 6:7). Jesus cautions His followers to "not be like them, for your Father knows what you need before you ask him" (Matthew 6:8).

NOTES

Instead, persistence in prayer simply means that we should develop the habit of prayer. What can be more exciting than having a continuing conversation with God? By relating this parable, Jesus is inviting us to persistently talk with our heavenly Father—not meaningless repetition of the same old formula prayer, but a deep and fruitful communication.

A young Christian who gets in the habit of talking with God will discover an exciting personal relationship with the Lord. Furthermore, that Christian will have established a pattern of seeking God in good times, which will serve him or her well when times get bad—when it's time to "cry out to him day and night" (Luke 18:7).

The Coming Bad Times

At the end of His parable, Jesus inquires rhetorically, "However, when the Son of Man comes, will he find faith on the earth?" (v. 8). He will if Christians persist in their communication and loyalty to Him. In Matthew 24:12,13 Jesus says, "Because of the increase of wickedness, the love of most will grow cold, but he who stands firm to the end will be saved." This passage is part of Jesus' great discourse on the end times, the time of Christ's reappearing. We know that we are saved by grace through faith (see Eph. 2:8); therefore we know that "he who stands firm to the end will be saved" (Matt. 24:13), not because he stood firm out of stubbornness, but out of faith. That is why Jesus asks if He will find faith when He returns—will people persist in their loyalty during hard times?

And that is why persistence in prayer and loyalty to God is so important. Not only is persistence a nice habit to get into now that it's relatively easy to be a Christian in our part of the world, but also in the future bad times when that persistence will be the key to spiritual endurance.

SESSION PLAN

BEFORE CLASS BEGINS: The OPTIONAL part of the ATTENTION GRABBER requires a bit of effort on your part before entering the classroom. Photocopy enough Parchment worksheets for each student to have one.

Attention Grabber

ATTENTION GRABBER: (2-3 minutes)

Here's a fun game to tip your students off to the subject of the lesson. The game is called "Monkey." The object of the game is for students to guess the word *pray*. The rules are simple:

1. Tell students, **I want you to guess the word I'm thinking of. I'm going to give you several sentences that contain the word, only instead of saying the actual word, I'm going to say the**

word *monkey*. **Feel free to ask questions and to try to guess the correct word.**

2. Say the first sentence, **I like to *monkey*.** Be sure students understand what they are supposed to do, and challenge them to guess the correct word as soon as they can. Use these sentences until someone identifies the word *pray*:

> **I like to *monkey* as often as I can.**
> **I *monkey* when I eat, and when I get up in the morning and go to bed at night.**
> **Sometimes I *monkey* quickly, sometimes I *monkey* for a long time.**
> **God likes my *monkeys*. In fact, He likes your *monkeys*, too.**
> **How often do you *monkey* to God?**
> **Does God answer your *monkeys*?**
> **What do you say to God when you *monkey*?**
> **To *monkey* means to talk to God.**

Someone will probably have guessed the correct answer by now. If not, tell students that the word is *pray* and thank them for their efforts.

OPTIONAL:

If you think your students are sharp enough, use the word *persistent* or *persistence* instead of *prayer*. Spend a few minutes to dream up several sentences to use as hints.

Make a transition to the EXPLORATION by saying something like, **The parable we will be looking at today is about an unjust judge and a widow who persisted in her cries for justice. The point of the parable is persistence in prayer and in loyalty to God.**

Bible Exploration

EXPLORATION (20-30 minutes)

Step 1 (8-10 minutes): Read Luke 18:2-8 aloud (or ask volunteers to read portions). Lead a class discussion based on information found in INSIGHTS FOR THE LEADER. Here are some suggested discussion questions:

Why did Jesus tell His disciples this parable? To show them they should always pray and not give up (see v. 1). **How did Jesus describe the judge?** The judge neither feared God nor cared about men (v. 2). **What did the widow want the judge to do?** Grant her justice against her adversary (v. 3). **Why do you suppose the widow had to come to the judge for justice?** Being a widow, she was without family for support, probably in bad financial straits, and defenseless against her adversary. **What did the judge do at first?** He refused her (v. 4). **Why did he end up granting her request?** Because she was bothering him with her persistence.

Read again verses 6-8 to your students. Say, **In comparing God to the judge, what differences do we see?** The judge is unjust and must be coerced into response—God is fair and quickly brings justice to His chosen ones. **What similarities are there?** The judge is in authority and has the power to grant requests. God is in ultimate control and has infinite power to answer prayer.

Now say something like this: **Verse 8 says that Jesus asked, "However, when the Son of Man**

comes, will he find faith on the earth?" Some of you may be wondering how Jesus' question relates to the rest of the story. It does relate, but in order to understand it, we must take a look at another part of the Bible. Turn in your Bibles to Matthew 24:12,13.

Point out that Matthew 24 is Jesus' description of the end times, the point in history revolving around His return to earth. Read verses 12,13 and say, **Because times will be hard, many people will grow cold and distant. But the one who persists in faith to God will be saved. So we see that the reason Jesus asked about faith on earth at His return is that many people won't be practicing persistent faith. His parable in Luke 18 is about persistence. The main point of His story is persistence in prayer, and here we see the importance of the kind of saving faith that brings a persistent love for God. Persistent prayer and persistent closeness to the Lord are vital keys to successful Christian living.**

Now have students follow along as you read Matthew 6:7,8. Say, **These two verses contrast with the parable Jesus told. In the parable, Jesus said to persist in praying to God. Here in Matthew 6, Jesus says to avoid repetition of the same old requests. Is there a contradiction here?** Allow students to respond, then point out that Matthew 6:7,8 is speaking of needless length of prayers (hoping to coerce God into answering with many arguments and reasons) and needless repetition (hoping to coerce God with persistent begging—which demonstrates a lack of faith in God's desire to answer.)

Say, **The parable is speaking about persisting in the *act* of prayer—not needless repetition of the same prayer. In other words, pray all the time, but don't get stuck on the same topic all the time. Develop the *habit of talking to God*. That's what He wants.**

Step 2 (8-10 minutes): Distribute the Parchment worksheet. Point out the section titled "Time for God." Read the instructions to the students and tell them to work individually or in pairs to complete the chart.

After everyone has completed the assignment, ask a few volunteers to describe how much time they spend doing certain activities such as watching TV, eating, or hanging out with friends. Then ask the entire class to express their opinion concerning the amount of time spent doing godly things (activities 12-14 on the chart) compared to the amount of time spent doing other things. The time spent with God will probably be tiny compared to the time spent doing other things.

Say, **There are two lessons we can learn from this chart. One, we tend to spend too little time with the One we claim to love and serve. We must commit ourselves to doing better. Two, if you think about it, you'll realize that all of the things listed on the chart can be done with God. For example, when we get up and get dressed, we can be thinking about the Lord. When we do homework, we can ask for Him to give us wisdom and understanding. At school, we can serve Him by the way we treat other students. Even sleeping, we can commit ourselves to Him as we drift off into dreamland.**

Step 3 (5-6 minutes): Lead a quick discussion on the nature of prayer (talking with God concerning requests, giving thanks, praising God, commitment to Him), the times and places to pray (anytime, anywhere), and the importance of praying for others as well as oneself.

Make a transition to the CONCLUSION by stressing the importance of each person's commitment to a regular, habitual prayer life.

Conclusion and Decision

CONCLUSION (3-5 minutes)

Tell students to individually and prayerfully complete the "Contract Between Me and Thee" section of the Parchment.

Allow students a few minutes to do the assignment. Encourage them to save their contracts and to display them on their walls for a time. Close in prayer and distribute the Fun Page.

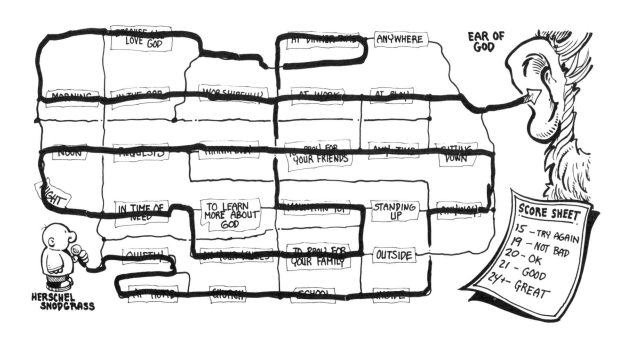

Your students may wish to see this solution to the Fun Page Puzzle.

(If you like, write the solution on an extra copy of the Fun Page and pin it to your classroom bulletin board.)

SESSION 13

Time for God

This chart represents a typical Monday in your life (during school time, not vacation time). Fill in the approximate number of hours you spend doing all the things listed. Then add up all the hours—they should come to about 24, or you need to try again.

ACTIVITY	AMOUNT OF TIME
1. Getting up and dressed.	
2. Personal hygiene (brushing teeth, bathing or showering, etc.).	
3. Fixing, eating and cleaning up after meals.	
4. School (with travel to and from).	
5. Homework.	
6. Job (with travel to and from).	
7. Chores at home.	
8. Listening to TV, music, etc.	
9. Sports and other active entertainment.	
10. Hanging out with friends.	
11. Reading for pleasure.	
12. Church activities.	
13. Personal Bible study.	
14. Personal prayer.	
15. Getting ready for bed.	
16. Sleep.	
17. Other things you think of (list).	

TOTAL HOURS (Should be 24.) _____

Contract Between Me and Thee

Dear God:

Thank you for prayer. I promise to develop the habit of daily prayer. Help me to remember to talk to you as often as possible. I will start a regular habit of prayer. I'll pray every day at (check one or more):

☐ Morning time
☐ Bedtime
☐ Other:

Signed: _____

Date: _____

WHERE, WHEN, WHY AND HOW

Session 13

Where, when, why and how should you talk to God? Everywhere, everywhere, everywhen, everywhy, and everyhow! To help you see what we're talking about, try this simple but challenging game.

Instructions: Put your pencil point on Herschel Snodgrass's microphone. Follow the wires to the Ear of God, trying to find the path with the largest numbers of answers to where, when, why and how to pray. You cannot cross your own path (except on wires that don't touch), and you cannot use the same section of wire twice. You'll want to erase your path and try several times. Compare your score to the Score Sheet below.

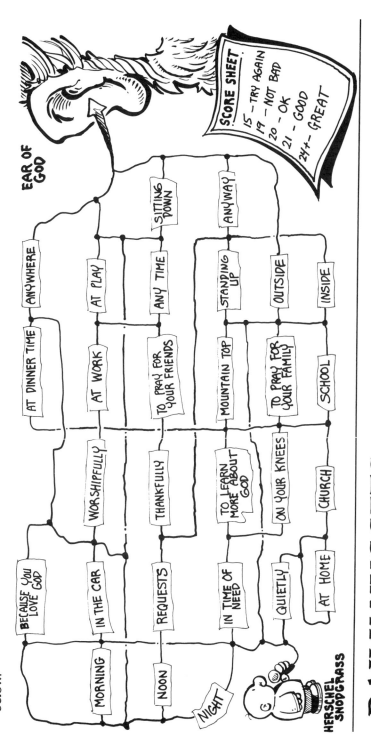

SCORE SHEET
15 – TRY AGAIN
19 – NOT BAD
20 – OK
21 – GOOD
24+ – GREAT

EAR OF GOD

HERSCHEL SNODGRASS

ANYWHERE · AT DINNER TIME · AT PLAY · AT WORK · WORSHIPFULLY · IN THE CAR · BECAUSE YOU LOVE GOD

SITTING DOWN · ANY TIME · TO PRAY FOR YOUR FRIENDS · THANKFULLY · REQUESTS · NOON · MORNING

ANYWAY · STANDING UP · MOUNTAIN TOP · TO LEARN MORE ABOUT GOD · IN TIME OF NEED · NIGHT

OUTSIDE · TO PRAY FOR YOUR FAMILY · ON YOUR KNEES · QUIETLY

INSIDE · SCHOOL · CHURCH · AT HOME

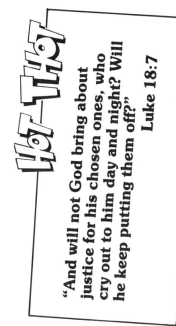

HOT-TIP

"And will not God bring about justice for his chosen ones, who cry out to him day and night? Will he keep putting them off?"

Luke 18:7

DAILY NUGGETS
Wisdom from God's Word for you to read each day.

Day 1 Read 1 Thessalonians 5:17. How is it possible to continually pray and still go about the business of the day?

Day 2 Psalm 37:4. What promise is made? What does "delight yourself in the Lord" mean?

Day 3 Colossians 4:2. To what are you supposed to devote yourself?

Day 4 Colossians 4:2. What two things are a part of prayer? What do you think we should watch for?

Day 5 Luke 11:1-4. What did the disciple ask Jesus to do?

Day 6 Luke 11:5-13. What good gift does God want to give to you (see verse 13)?

THEME: The habit of prayer pays off.

Session 13

BIBLE STUDY OUTLINE

Read Luke 11:5-13 to your students, making the following points as time allows.

- VERSES 5-8: Jesus tells His followers a story about a lazy man who didn't want to get out of bed to lend his friend three loaves of bread. But the moocher persists and eventually the lazy man gets rid of him by giving him the bread.
- VERSES 9,10: Jesus then makes a fantastic promise to His listeners, which can be summed up, "God answers prayer!" Notice that to receive an answer to prayer, a person must ask, seek and knock. In other words, we should be in a habit of coming to God in prayer if we want to receive His answers. A Christian who doesn't pray will miss out.

  Prayer can be several things. It can be requests for things we need or want, it can be thanksgiving for a blessing, it can be praise to Him. Prayer can be just a simple conversation with the Lord, or a deeply emotional struggle during a time of personal tragedy or some other crisis. It's important to develop a habit of talking with God—in fact, it's a responsibility as well as a privilege. God expects to hear from us. He wants to answer our prayers.
- VERSES 11-13. Now Jesus contrasts the love of God with the lazy man who didn't want to answer his friend's request. Jesus makes His point by using an absurd illustration: fathers giving their sons dangerous snakes and scorpions when they ask for food. Even evil, dim-witted human beings don't do that. So how much more will our loving heavenly Father be glad to give us good gifts—even the gift of the Holy Spirit to live inside of us!

STORY: ANSWERED PRAYER

We suggest you tell your listeners about several of your experiences with answered prayer. Close your message by encouraging students to develop a daily routine of spending at least 5-10 minutes in prayer at a set time each day. Allow students a moment to privately determine what time they will pray (recommend morning time before the day begins and/or bedtime).

DISCUSSION QUESTIONS

1. **What is prayer? What are some of the things Christians your age should be regularly praying about?**

2. **Jesus said that anyone who asks, seeks or knocks will find. Is there any Christian who is an exception to this promise?**

3. **Is there anything that could stand between a Christian and answered prayer? If so, what could be done about it?**

4. **Why do you think Jesus placed such an emphasis on the gift of the Holy Spirit?**

5. **What are some of your experiences with answered prayer?**

THE COMPLETE
JUNIOR HIGH BIBLE STUDY
RESOURCE BOOK #3

Three ways to introduce the members of a group.

NAME SCRAMBLE

Students form pairs. The participants in each pair combine the letters in their first and last names to form as many words as possible. Words must be three or more letters. The pair with the most words after a set time limit wins.

STRING ME ALONG

Each participant ties a long string to his or her finger. The strings should be 15 to 20 feet long. The leader grabs the strings into a bundle as shown, and allows each participant to choose an end of string. The leader releases the string, and each participant follows the string he or she holds to the person on the other end. If a person is tied to him or herself, he or she must try again.

Players then get to know each other.

MAP-PLE PIE

Before your game time begins, plot the addresses of your meeting's "regulars" on a map (by drawing a dot at each address). If visitors show up at the meeting, get their addresses on a sign-up sheet and quickly plot the addresses on the map. Cut the map into pieces, one dot per piece if possible. Put the pieces in a hat or other container. Participants draw pieces (making sure they don't take their own addresses). Each participant must then find out who the address on his or her piece belongs to and write that person's name next to the dot. Participants then gather together to glue the map pieces to a poster board.

CLIP ART AND OTHER GOODIES

The following pages contain all sorts of fun, high quality clip art. Put it to good use: brighten up your youth group's mail outs, bulletins, posters and overhead transparencies. Cut 'em out, paste 'em up, run 'em off and there you have it!

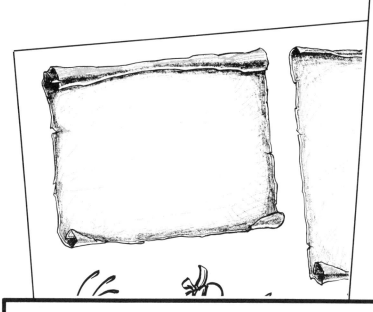

WANT TO PRODUCE GREAT PROMOTIONAL MATERIAL?

TURN THE PAGE FOR EASY INSTRUCTIONS...

EASY INSTRUCTIONS

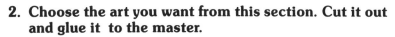

1. Get a sheet of clean white paper. This will be the master for your promotional piece.

2. Choose the art you want from this section. Cut it out and glue it to the master.

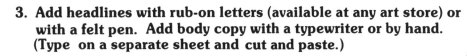

3. Add headlines with rub-on letters (available at any art store) or with a felt pen. Add body copy with a typewriter or by hand. (Type on a separate sheet and cut and paste.)

4. Run off as many copies as you need, hand them out or drop them in the mail. Presto!

TIPS:

Go heavy on the artwork, light on the copy. A piece with too many words goes unread.

Get in the habit of making a monthly calendar of events. It doesn't have to be an expensive masterpiece; just so it tells your group members what they can find at your church.

Print the calendar on the back of the student worksheet or the takehome paper. This will insure that these pages are saved and read.

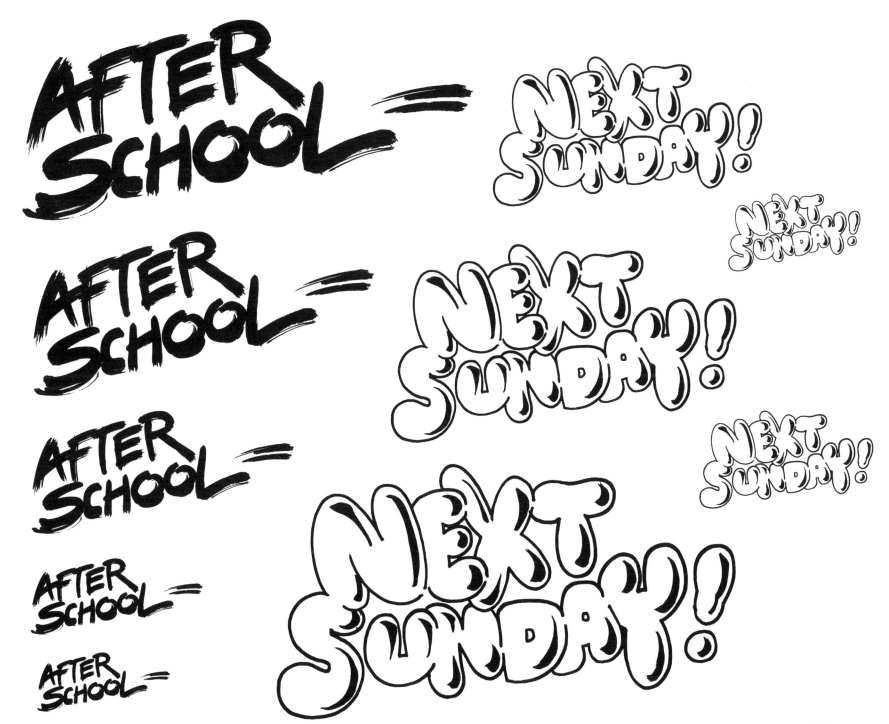

159

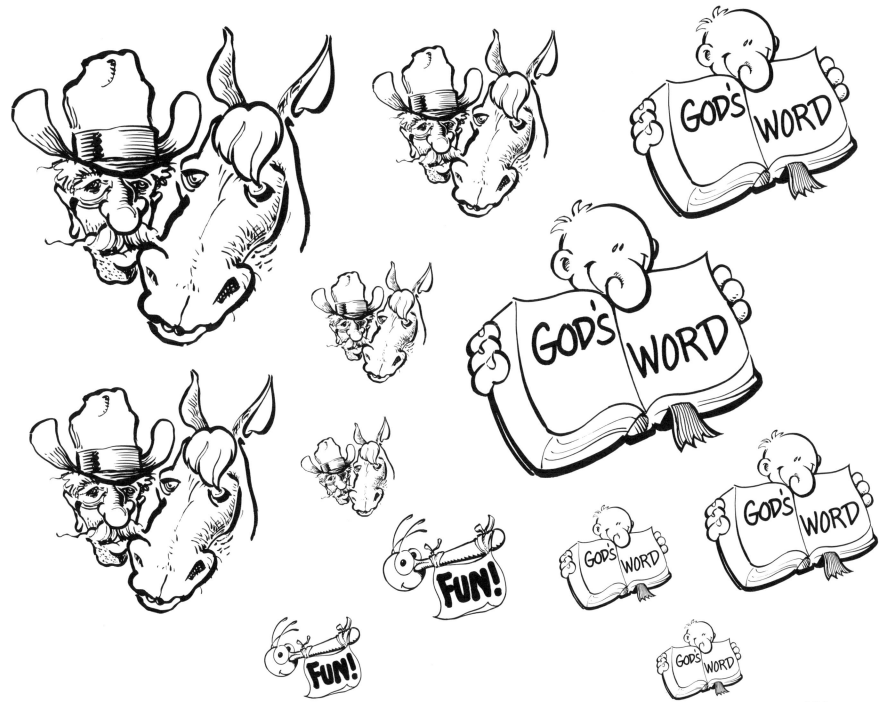